Wine Routes of
PENEDÈS

and

CATALONIA

OTHER BOOKS BY ALAN YOUNG

An Encounter With Wine
(Wine Information Bureau, Perth 1977)
new edition 1986

Australian Wines and Wineries
(Horwitz Grahame, Sydney 1983)

Australia-New Zealand Wine Year Book
(International Wine Academy 1986)

Making Sense of Wine -
A Study in Sensory Perception
(Greenhouse Publications, 1986)
new editions 1989, 1995

Making Sense of Wine Tasting
(Lennard Books, London 1987)

Chardonnay - The Definitive Guide
(Sidgwick & Jackson, London 1988)
new edition 1989
(International Wine Academy, 1991)
new edition 1994

Wine is Fun!
(International Wine Academy, 1995)
Chinese Edition 1998

Wine Routes of Argentina
(International Wine Academy, 1998)

Wine Routes of
PENEDÈS

and

CATALONIA

Alan Young

Contributing Writer
Harold Heckle

INTERNATIONAL
WINE ACADEMY
SAN FRANCISCO
SYDNEY

First published in 2000 by

International Wine Academy

38 Portola Drive

San Francisco CA USA 94131

Fax: 1 415 641 7348

ayoung@sirius.com

19 Boronia Ave Winmalee

NSW 2777 Australia

Cover design by Tony Cooper, Madras Neils

Maps by Gary Chen & Alan Young

Set in 11pt Garamond

Library of Congess Catalogue Card

ISBN 0-9596983-4-5

Distributed in the UK by

Drake International Services

Tel: 44 1869 338240

email: info@drakeint.co.uk

Distributed in the USA by

International Wine Academy

1 800 345 8466

Fax: 1 415 641 7348

email: ayoung@sirius.com

CONTENTS

DEDICATION

To the legion of Catalan winegrowers who
love their land, their language, their wine
and their food.
Also to Alberto, Andrea, Norma, Tony and
Wendy.

DENOMINACIÓ D'ORIGEN CATALUNYA

The creation of the new D.O. Catalunya was approved on December 1, 1999, along with it corresponding regulations.

The creation of this Denomination of Origin addresses the need toclarify and defend the typicity of Catalan Denominations of Origin. It had become clear that it was necessary to apply a pyramidal concept of Denomination of Origin within an autonomous community with nine producing regions. This is to say that a new qualitative level was needed to encompass, on the one hand, wines made from grapes originatingfrom different Catalan Denominations of Origin, while at the same time maintaining the already existing Denominations of Origin as the maximum reference points for the quality and typicity of these wines.

The appearance of this new quality level (the base of a pyramidal structure) will reinforce the superior level, that of the already existing nine Denominations of Origin, each corresponding to concrete geographical regions.

Wines that do not manage to achieve the requirements of these pre-existing Denominations of Origin will go on to be encompassed within this new, generic Denomination of Origin.

The Denomination of Origin Catalunya will take in 60,000 hectares,within 335 municipalities that have traditionally cultivated vines.

FOREWORD

When Catalonia was first settled, the world was flat and the ends of the earth were the extremes of the Mediterranean. Today much has changed. Supertankers and giant aircraft bring every part of the world, and millions of people, to the ports and airports of Catalonia.

Yet, much has not changed over the centuries. As a general rule, Catalans nowadays are happy with a simple way of life - riding a bicycle, swimming, sailing, hunting or fishing on weekends and a siesta after the main meal of the day, lunch. Yes, most of Catalonia still closes from 1pm-4pm for a long lunch and rest break and then back to work until, possibly 8pm. There is much to commend this sensible way of life, especially on a hot summer's afternoon.

In the evenings the town rambla is a community gathering place, where folks young and old, meet and chat or visit with each other or, maybe, have a game of checkers; a very civilized life style.

Catalonia is a unique place, like nothing else in Spain. There are few bullfights, the language is its own and the work ethic is strong. Blessed with a very livable climate Catalonia has one boundary that is the formidable Mediterranean, and provider of superb seafood which everyone seems to prepare exquisitely.

Despite the government's legalized robbery conducted through autopista toll charges — so numerous that it seems to defeat the purpose of a non-stop highway, travel in Catalonia is a pleasant experience. However, many road signs are extremely confusing for visitors, a reason that we spent much time preparing the first-ever accurate guide maps to the wine regions.

Vilafranca del Penedès is a very special place, big enough to have every modern amenity, small enough to still be a country town. It is no problem to walk anywhere in the town. Good restaurants abound and, of course, the wines are superb and great value. It is only a short drive to a number of good beaches, or forests, or the many other amenities that the visitor may desire. Vilafranca is a perfect base for exploring one of the world's fastest emerging wine regions. This book is strongly oriented towards Penedès - and for a very good reason. A group of Penedès wineries paid for the printing of this work as a promotion for their region and generously agreed to allow 12 pages for other Catalan wine regions.

Being an Australian based in California with few Spanish language skills, this work has been an interesting challenge. Yet, visiting Catalonia, language was rarely a problem as most people in the wine business speak English and many are fluent in French or German.

Catalonia is a cultural wonderland. Artists of every description abound here, singers like José Carreras and Montserrat Caballé, famous painters such as Joan Miró, Pablo Picasso, Salvador Dalí, Antonio Tapias and Miguel Barceló to name but a few. This was also home to the great cellist Pablo Casals and, of course, the architect Antonio Gaudí and his disciples. Craft people of every calling will offer their goods and services in every corner of this great country.

It is all here - just waiting for you to come and visit.

9

ACKNOWLEDGEMENTS

Although there is but one author who may receive the plaudits, it takes many people to produce a book. Recognising the unique focus of the book, the publishers made an international search for a contributing writer with wide experience in Spain, Catalonia in particular, and a deep knowledge of their customs and culture. We found the exact person in Bristol, U.K. in the form of Harold Heckle who has contributed 20 percent of the book's material.

Then there are the entrepreneurs who were prepared to gamble on the book's success, in this regard two people were outstanding - Josep Ribas, Director of the Consejo Regulador Penedès and Joan Gil Secretary-Director of UVIPE - without whose efforts this book would never have happened.

The book was wholly produced in San Francisco by the staff and friends of the International Wine Academy; the friends doing the bulk of the work! Tony and Wendy Cooper made the computer understand what we were trying to piece together, Tony with his computer wizardry and artistic grace - Wendy the lady of words, sometimes called an honorary editor.

Gary Chen produced the maps and the other computer generated artwork. Norma Young and Andrea Klein contributed much about the history and art - in words and photos - and the Index.

There were many people all over Catalonia who provided friendship, information, meals and courtesies too numerous to mention but I am sure they know who I mean. However, we would be remiss not to single-out Alberto Fornos, public relations whiz, friend and man for all occasions. José and Silvia Puig and Antonio Pont were also generous in their support - along with many other kind people including the staff of the Hotel Domo. A special thanks also to Bodegas Oliveda in Capmany for allowing the use of the border of their label to surround the map on the cover.

Jan Read and Maite Manjón very kindly allowed us to reproduce recipes from their splendid book *CATALONIA Traditions, Places, Wine and Food,* absolutely recommended reading for visitors to the region. The chef and owner of Restaurant Ca la Katy, Sant Marti Sarroca, prepared the food and arranged the food photography - a sterling performance.

Thank you all.

PREFACE

Catalonia is well known throughout the world for its famous sparkling wine, *cava*. The sheer volume and visibility of cava in the world's markets tends to diminish the excellence of the region's less publicized still wines.

This book therefore, will be devoted only to the still wines of Penedès (and other Catalan regions), even though many of the still wines are made by the cava houses. The decision was made to investigate these superlative and exciting wines by the author, the publisher - International Wine Academy - and two local entities - the Consejo Regulador (regulating council) and Unió Vinícola del Penedès, an association of wineries.

Although the author and contributing writer have had a lengthy and relatively close association with Catalonia through teaching and writing about its wine, we could not have anticipated how little we knew about Penedès when it came to magnifying the area in depth. A single region has given rise to a work larger than most books about the whole of Spain.

During this work we discovered a staggering well of virtually unknown and excellent wines, favourably priced to compete with the world's best. This is the information we hope to convey to you, the reader. This book will reveal much new and scientifically fresh information that should appeal to lovers of good wine, food and history.

Using Vilafranca del Penedès as the base, I have divided the Penedès region into convenient routes to cater for the serious wine lover or collector, and have also devised these routes to appeal to those discerning tourists who combine a love of wine and exquisite food with an appreciation for archeological, architectural and historical panoramas, not to mention astoundingly beautiful landscapes. These are presented with maps and particular points of interest.

Catalan wines quenched the thirst of Imperial Rome and are as old as history, but their "new" protagonism only came to life in the 1960s and 70s, due mainly to the pioneering work of Miguel A. Torres, Jean Leon and others. They brought the vines of France and the know-how and technology of France and California to the region. Theirs, alone, is an incredible story.

In the fast changing world of our third millennium, the people of Penedès understand that they cannot stand still to realise a vision of the future. Unions, regulating bodies, bodegas and grape growers are all banding together to look into the crystal ball and plan for the future of the region in the next decade. Everything will be on the table: export markets, viticulture, technical training, equipment - nothing will be left unturned.

This is the Catalonia that was rediscovered, a thriving, innovative and creative land, blessed with dedicated, intelligent and articulate people. Please join in touring one of the world's most beautiful and rewarding wine countries.

Cheers!, ¡Salud!, ¡Salut!

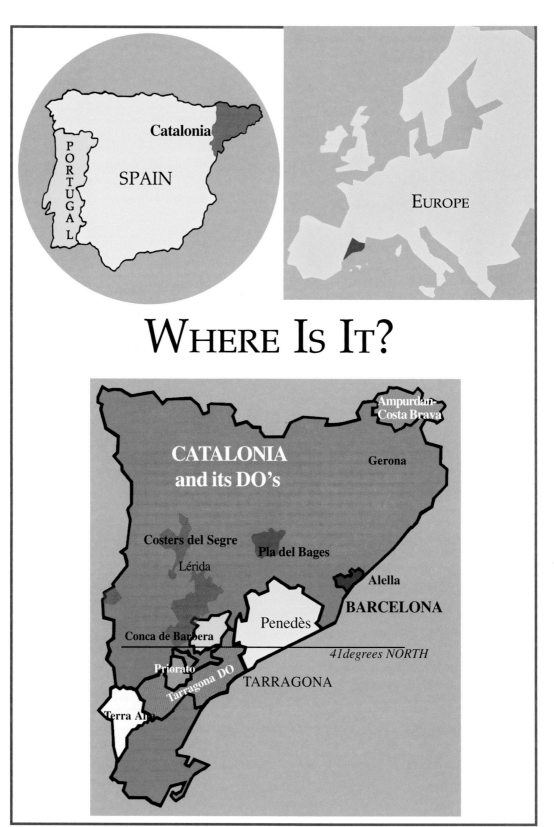

WHERE IS IT?

A Little Penedès History

This could be a book about history, Catalonia and Penedès are so rich with it; history is there at every corner, building and farm. Catalonia has its own language and government autonomy - and the people are atypically Spanish. In fact, their language is spoken in the south of France with whom the Catalans have, historically, had greater ties than with Madrid.

The Catalan language is not a Spanish dialect - rather a "popular" Latin. History records Catalans as being a proud, industrious and stubborn people.

During the 8th - 6th centuries BC, the Phoenicians (by their discovery of the Pole Star), along with their Carthaginian friends, sailed and traded the whole of the Mediterranean. The Phoenicians were Eastern Mediterranean people of Semite tongue, who we know today as the occupants of Lebanon, Syria and Israel. The Carthaginians, in particular, made inroads to the Catalan coast in the western Mediterranean establishing trading posts at Tarragona and Barcelona.

Recent archeological studies have literally unearthed a volume of new information which is in the process of re-writing the history of wine in Europe. This research continues to reveal new knowledge as the information is being processed. The work indicates that the vine was well-established and thriving in the region, and indeed well into the heartland of the Iberian Peninsula, in early Iberian times, maybe a thousand years before the coming of the Phoenicians.

What this suggests is that wine culture migrated with greater ease than previously thought, and that early traders spread a sophisticated system for cultivating vines and producing wine. It was the Phoenicians' mastery of this agricultural art

- perhaps aided by new vine species and vineyard knowledge - that has allowed them to be recorded in history as the forefathers of today's global wine industry.

However, it was the Romans who developed vine culture, probably starting about 197BC, in Catalonia. For seven centuries the Romans made Catalonia the centre of Roman Hispania. Evidence of the Roman occupation and influence is there for all to see, and wonder at, in the 21st century. The Romans also brought religion, lifestyle, including many culinary styles, incredible road and bridge construction, and, the language. Many parts of the famous Via Augusta road, from Cadiz to Rome, are still in use more than 2,000 years later.

The magnificent wine museum at Vilafranca del Penedès, just 40 km west of Barcelona, contains documents and amphorae that takes the region's vine history back to the 4th century BC but it was the end of the warring era that allowed the settlement of farms and organized wine growing.

Ever since those Roman days, the Catalans have had an ongoing, uphill battle in a country not blessed with a largesse of minerals or natural riches - other than three wonderful harbours - Barcelona, Tarragona and Vilanova i la Geltrú (built in 1949), good farming land, a benevolent climate and diligent people.

Over the centuries, a continuous stream of invaders from the north, south, east and within, came and selectively tried to destroy the land, the culture and the vines.

After the Romans came the Goths in the 5th century. Then in 712 the conquering Moslem

Moors came from North Africa and stayed until the 15th century. Due to the Moslem religion, this was a disastrous period for wine growers. Charlemagne reconquered Barcelona in 801 to establish a Frankish outpost and his Marca Hispanica- a region also embracing Aragón.

This settlement established a strong defensive line between the Christians in the north (France) and the Moors in the south. About this time the Catalan language became accepted in the area. For the next 200 years battles raged in what we might today call the Penedès Valley, forcing the inhabitants to abandon their farms and vines and depart for safer places.

The slow re-population of the Valley was hastened when the Counts of Barcelona became involved by building a series of outstanding castles, a number of them still standing today: Olerdola built 929, Subirats 943, La Granada (950), Gelida (963), Vallformosa (977) and Sant Marti Sarroca (986). These castles attracted re-habitation of the villages which, inevitably, brought about a feudal system leading to fighting and, subsequently, evacuation to other places like Vilafranca del Penedès circa 1108, and seaside villages such as Vilanova.

In the 14th century, King Juan 2 declared war on Vilafranca which had sided with Prince Carlos de Vienna. King Juan was victorious and made the locals sign the *Capitulation of Vilafranca*. A series of monstrous events followed, beginning with the Great plague which killed many throughout Europe. This was followed by a plague of a different kind, locusts from North Africa which devoured everything standing in the fields.

Invariably, the Catalans ignored the Castillian monarchy and sided with outsiders rather than the monarchy and too often ended-up on the losing side. Often these losses prejudiced their hopes of autonomy and their beloved language. Even in the 20th century Catalans regained self-government in 1932 only to see Franco and his civil war remove government to Madrid once more. Autonomy was regained in 1977 with control over four provinces, those of Barcelona, Gerona, Lèrida and Tarragona.

The people of Penedès have bounced along the road of history, surviving one crisis after another. Today there appears an assured future with great prospects for all.

The Roman amphitheatre, where Christians were fed to African lions, overlooks the port of Tarragona, a starting point for much of Catalonia's greatness. Now the port is home to super tankers.

A STARTLING DISCOVERY

Some years ago, a discovery made by a group of archaeologists working on a beautiful hilltop on the Mediterranean coast of Spain not far from Denia began to change well-established perceptions about the past. History and the past are, despite our best efforts, always a bit of a mystery, and certainly far from a precise science. What this discovery revealed were ancient traces of a reasonably sophisticated wine culture that seemed to antedate the previously accepted times for the introduction of winemaking into western Europe.

The site was given the name of L'Alt de Benimaquia. It contained a hill fort, a reasonably sizeable town, grain and general food stores, and convincing evidence of a complex wine-making operation. The problem lay in its antiquity. It all appeared to be older than recognised orthodoxy would allow. Historians have always believed that wine, and the grapevine, travelled to western Europe with Phoenician traders. They are credited with having spread the three varietal columns on which modern winemaking is based; *Vitis vinifera pontica*, *Vitis vinifera occidentalis* and *Vitis vinifera orientalis*; from Tyre to Cádiz along the Mediterranean.

What the archeological discovery at L'Alt de Benimaquia suggests is that some kind of wine culture had already been implanted in southern Spain by Phoenician times, and that it might have become even more sophisticated with the long-term trading links to the Middle East that they provided. The evidence thrown up by this mysterious and haunting hilltop dig might have remained an unusual and inexplicable aberration had it not been for another surprising discovery. This time the dig was not on the coast, near sea-borne trading routes, it was slap bang in the middle of Spain, in Valdepeñas, due south of Madrid.

While excavating at Cerro de las Cabezas, archeologist Dr Javier Pérez Avilés came across evidence of an Iberian city. Digging down, ever more ancient remains were revealed. At the strata levels equivalent to 500 BC, he discovered substantial amounts of Phoenician ceramics and artifacts. Digging further down, reaching the strata levels pertinent to 700 BC he found, much as the archaeologists near Denia, evidence of complex wine-making facilities. Dr Pérez Avilés has yet to dig further down. The site is still a new discovery, and progress is being made methodically, slowly and carefully.

On the face of it, a body of material is coming to light to suggest that Iberian people had been exposed to the cultivation of the vine and to winemaking techniques sufficiently in advance of the earliest Phoenician times for quite advanced practices to have reached the very heart of Spain by the earliest Phoenician settlement dates. Who knows what further evidence of wine's past in Europe may yet be uncovered in the future?

One thing is certain, southern and south eastern Spain have played a key role in the dissemination of wine culture in western Europe. The early introduction, via the Ebro Valley, of Vitis vinifera pontica has led to the birth of Europe's best white grape varieties. Vitis vinifera occidentalis is the precursor of the best red varieties, including almost certainly Pinot noir and Cabernet Sauvignon.

While French men (or rather Gauls) were exchanging goods and valuables (even their women, according to Julius Caesar) with the Romans for wine, ports on the Catalan coast were exporting wines to other parts of the Roman world. The grape varieties brought over by Phoenician (and, who knows, maybe even pre-Phoenician, if the evidence is correct) traders certainly took to their new homeland with *gusto*. The region known today as Catalonia (or Catalunya in Catalan, Cataluña in Spanish, Catalogne in French) certainly deserves recognition for the role it has played in bringing wine to us today. Many of the varieties and blends of varieties that have become so fashionable and trendy today descend from the early varieties brought to Europe via its coast. Garnacha, Cariñena, Monastrell, (Grenache, Carignan and Mourvèdre in French) are all native Catalan and Aragonese varieties.

Having said that, the region did go through two periods of considerable difficulty in terms of wine production. The first appears around about the second century AD, when winemaking seems to have come to all but a complete halt in the region. The next was with the arrival of phylloxera. There is little or no evidence to point to a cause for the first decline in production. What is clear is that wine-related materials decreased dramatically in numbers. The catastrophe provoked by phylloxera is hard to exaggerate.

The Industrial Revolution had brought great wealth to the sections of French society most likely to spend on good quality wines. The arrival of phylloxera in France in 1863 caused a near collapse in the making of wine just as the market was booming. Ever aware of a sensible commercial potential, the Catalans recognised that here was a market desperate for a product they could clearly supply. What began as a trickle soon turned into a torrent as Catalan wine won not only French markets, but also those international ones traditionally supplied by the French. Such was the confidence that this new-found trade inspired that vast and exaggerated amounts of Catalan agriculture threw over their traditional crops in favour of the vine. The only problem lay in the optimistic expectation that phylloxera would not be hardy enough to cross the Pyrennees Mountains, that the mountains would act as a permanent barrier to the little insect.

The arrival of railways, in 1865, made the job of transporting wines to port even easier, convincing Catalan growers of the wisdom of their enterprise. This was the dawn of a new agricultural practice. For the first time, winemaking began to take on aspects of the industrial age. Then, in 1887 the horrible realisation that phylloxera had finally arrived, struck. At a steady speed of 20 kilometres a year it advanced on all the vineyards of Catalonia and, to put it bluntly, devastated them. Such had been the rate of conversion to viticulture that Catalan farmers, and more particularly, farm labourers, had few edible crops to turn to when the vineyards ceased to produce.

Hunger turned to starvation and destitution. Moving accounts of the time tell of how entire families made do with one cod fish a week, and whatever bread could be obtained. This was a blow that would take a long time to overcome, and forget. To this day you can still see evidence of the devastation wrought by the little mite in the way the Catalan landscape was reorganised to cope with the disaster of phylloxera. New crops and new farming systems were quickly brought in to try and arrest the devastation caused by phylloxera.

THREE UNLOVED AMERICANS

These days we understand that the bugs and bacteria which affect our very lives are minuscule things mainly invisible to the human eye. This micro world was virtually unknown in the mid 19th century at a time when the vineyards of France literally died. In fact, it was at this very time that Louis Pasteur became the person to unravel the wonders of fermentation during his superb research. Among his other discoveries was the system of *pasteurization* that saved France from an immense vinous disaster; and made the world's milk bacteria free.

In 1870 France was a net exporter of wine at an amazing eight-to-one ratio - for every litre of wine imported, France exported eight litres. By 1880 vines were dying all over the country and France a net importer at a three-to-one ratio. By 1887 France was importing wine at a ratio of six-to-one. Whatever could have caused this fourteen-one turn-around for France to move from a net exporter - to a net importer in just 17 years? Due to its close proximity, Spain became the main beneficiary of the export bonus.

One could say it was the invention of the steamship but that would be only half of the story. Steamships enabled American plant life to be transferred to Europe in a matter of days instead of weeks sailing ships took for the journey across the Atlantic. This faster time enabled diseases and pests to survive the trip and make the inter-continental connection, and America was generous in its export of vinous "nasties."

The most destructive pest destroying vines was an aphid previously unnamed due to an amazing set of circumstances. Vines were not only dy-

ing in France, this mysterious whatever had wiped out all attempts to establish European vines in the English settlements of east coast North America. It even struck down the precious vines of President Thomas Jefferson at Monticello, Virginia. But nobody understood what was happening; just a shake of the head and forget about such happenings. Not so in France, where wine was an export of such national pride that King Louis-Napoleon demanded answers.

In the first year of attack the invisible louse establishes itself on the vine's roots, next year the vines look "consumptive" —weak and without vigour; next year dead! Some vines could be pulled straight out of the ground without a problem - they had no roots! This gave the bug a three year start against detection and five years before anyone took action.

Jules-Emile Planchon, an enthusiastic amateur entomologist and professor of chemistry at Montpellier University, was one of hundreds of academics and researchers consulted. With magnification he could see the hordes of little yellow bugs on the roots of still-living vines and was knowledgeable enough to realize that this was the louse stage and that it must have a winged phase. From the winged bugs he found the tell-tale galls on the leaves of vines and identified them as being similar to phylloxera *quercas* which had caused problems also in European oak trees. Planchon then named this louse phylloxera *vastarix*, the devastator!

Having identified the problem, the next questions was: where did it come from? Reasoning suggested that if it was of European origin it would have wiped out the vines years before. Therefore, it must be a foreigner.

The first of the three American-introduced nasties, powdery mildew or *oïdium*, had made its French debut in 1847 and by 1854 the country had its worst, i.e. lowest and poorest, vintage for 70 years. (It came to Catalonia in the mid 1850s). Immediately prior to the phylloxera outbreak, there were many complaints from export customers about the watery, insipid quality of French wine. Louis-Napoleon summoned Pasteur. He demanded that the eminent scientist conduct immediate enquiries into the complaints of why the wines were so poor.

Under the right conditions, oïdium is a fast-developing airborne mildew fungus that stifles vine growth and berry colour development resulting in low crops and off-flavoured wines.

Then when phylloxera struck at the very tender heart of France's viticultural disasters, entomologists at England's Kew Gardens offered assistance. They had lengthy experience with American plant diseases and helped with reasoning that phylloxera was an American import.

Then came "The Cures" for phylloxera - or more aptly, the disasters of free-thinking! Between 1875 and 1889 French wine production dropped by a colossal 90 percent - and everyone had their answer to the problem. The solutions ranged from putting a living toad under each of the country's 11 billion vines - to flooding vineyards with white wine! (Can one, possibly, imagine the concept of flooding the Rhine or Loire Valleys?)

An even more crazy ground-injection system with liquid carbon bi-sulphide (using a PAL instrument illustrated) went into long-term operation. This required the injection of gas into 30,000 holes per hectare (2.47 acres) for the 68,000 ha (168,000 acres) being treated, and some vineyards continued this nonsense until the end of WW2. 30,000 times 68,000 equals 2,040,000,000, well, many holes! But this was only the start of a statistical exercise that cost millions of everything. For France alone, two million miles of vine material for grafting would be required from the US!

Grafting was the more scientific and rational approach. Mating the European vine trunk with the *tolerant* (NOT resistant) roots of the American vines was an idea that did not sit well with many French traditionalists. At the end of the 60s Planchon went to the blight's homeland to study the prospects of grafting the American vine - and to examine the acid soils which were different to Europe's alkaline soils. These soil types proved to be an early obstacle for viticulturists who were entering an entirely new phase of vine culture; many American vines refused to grow in the soils of Europe. Native American vines are complex, having attributes individual to the many regions from which they frequent - from Texas to Canada. Literally hundreds of thousands of vine crosses were made trying to find the right combination for phylloxera tolerance which varied with each crossing. Today, viticulturists can graft perfect mates for any need, but in the beginning it was all an experiment being addressed continents apart.

The first Spanish outbreak of phylloxera was found at Malaga in 1878, then Jerez 1894, Catalonia circa 1879 (Vilafranca del Penedès1887), and by this time vine breeders in France and the USA were getting on top of the horrific situation. This did not stop an almost complete destruction of Catalonian vineyards.

Local farmers did not need any more hassles; for centuries they had reeled from one disaster to another. Already in the 19th century they had survived the War of the Frenchmen and the Seven Years War, then nature took its toll with the introduction via France of oïdium; and now another French/American invader—phylloxera. As resilient as ever, the farmers not only imported American rootstocks for their own use but, indeed, became the supply house for all of Spain.

Fortunately these problems had hit France first and the resources of the viticultural world helped with a reasonably rapid recovery. The following decade were days in the sun for Catalan growers with exports flourishing, particularly to France, other European countries and the Americas.

Nasty number three, *downy* mildew (*peronospora*), brought about by humidity and summer rains, came on the roots of the American rootstocks that were the salvation from phylloxera. This fungus reduces crop yields and makes for poor wine. Fortunately the University of Bordeaux took only four years - forever to a politician, but nothing in the life of a viticulturist - to introduce the "Bordeaux Mixture" of copper, bi-sulphide and lime which you can see as a vivid blue spray on vines - and also home gardens around the world.

As roses are of the same family as grape vines, many vineyards grow roses at the ends of the vine rows. Fortuitously, roses attract mildew about two-three weeks ahead of the vines; an old-fashioned early-warning system.

After two or five millenniums of grape growing, the period of the three Unloved Americans in European vineyards did do something very positive. Dealing with the nasties took much of the tradition out of wine - and replaced it with a very new science . It was simply a case of back to square one for all. Today, Catalonia is on top of all these problems and its vineyards are looking magnificent.

Much of the credit for pioneering the rootstocks that eventually became the real cure for phylloxera is attributed to four beloved Americans in what could be called "strange" places. Dr.

Thomas Munson in Denison, Texas, USA, C.V. Riley, and two Missourans. Professor Husman of St. Louis and Herman Jaeger of Neosho.

Each received many awards from the French for their meritorious service, including the Legion of Honour. Statues are erected in honour of the men in at least two French towns. In 1996, Neosho MO citizens included Jaeger in their Walk of Honor with a statue (left) and the inscription is detailed below.

Herman Jaeger, a Swiss immigrant settled six miles east of Neosho (Missouri, USA) in 1865 and started a vineyard. He located superior wild grape vines in the area. Some of these local resistant varieties he sent to France in the 1870s. They were used to replenish the French vineyards which had been infected by a grape louse. In 1889 he was awarded the French Legion of Honor.

THREE REGIONS OF PENEDÈS

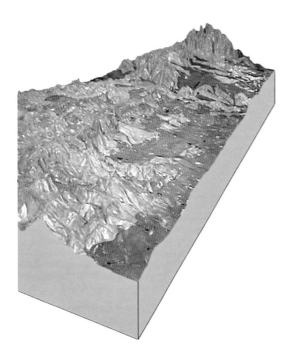

Upper Penedès *viticultural areas are 500-800 metres above sea level which makes the region ideal for northern European varieties and Parellada. Embraces the towns of San Martí de Sarroca, Font Rubi, Pontons, Pierola, Torrelles de Foix, Jaume S - Piera, Cabrera d'Anoia, Sant Q. de Mediona, La Llacuna, Miralles, Montmell, Aiguamurcia and Pla de Manlleu.*

With rolling plains ranging from 200 - 400m above sea level **Penedès Valley** *revolves around the capital, Vilafranca del Penedès. The region provides 60% of all grape production.*

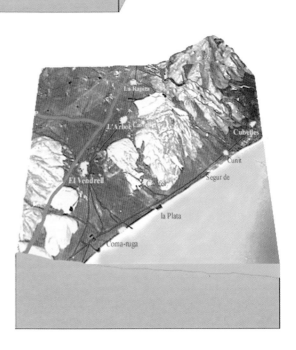

Vilanova i Geltrú is the capital of **Maritime Penedès** *which takes in many of the famous beach resorts including Sitges, Vilanova and Canyelles. Other wine producing villages are Llorenç del Penedès and Sant Jaume dels Domenys, El Vendrell, L'Arboç & Calafell.*
It is also home to the important white Macabeo grape - local red grapes also thrive in this warm region.

20

The Landscape

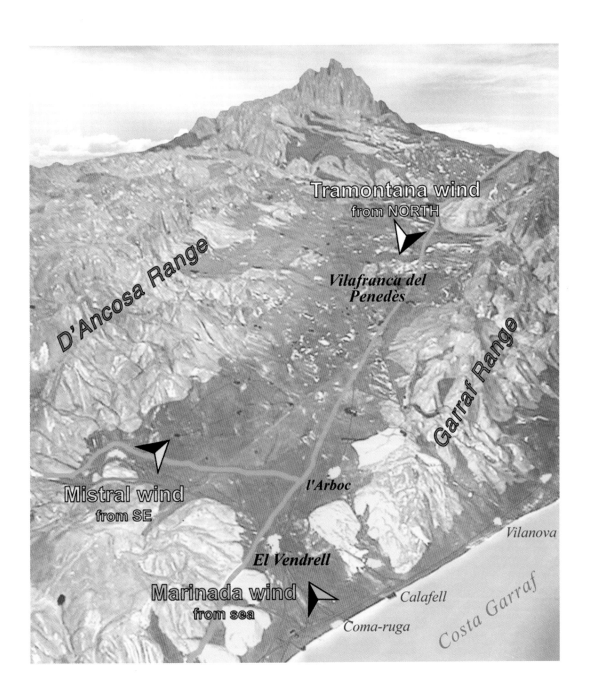

Penedès depression - with five-to-one vertical exaggeration - showing wind directions.

THE LANDSCAPE

The Penedès Valley - officially known as the Penedès Depression - is mainly from the quartenary period of geology, dating back three million years, however it is reasonable to say that most of the material was placed about 10,000 years ago (see map page 21). The foothills are mainly younger portions of the Cenozoic age, probably 27 million years old, while the more elevated points in the area are from the Cretacious period stretching back some 150 million years.

The highest visible points belong to the Jurassic (215 million years) and the Granitoid portion of the Palezoic age - up to 500 million years distant. Montserrat (serrated mountain), the icon of Catalonia, at the northern end of the valley, is probably 70 million years of age. The valley is an off-shoot of the impressive Pyrenees mountain range. Today, this mountain spectacle forms the northern boundary for both Spain and Catalonia.

Catalonia, like most other places, is a unique landscape. If anything, it is something like California, or, maybe Chile. All have a continuous coastline, mostly Mediterranean climate, with closely adjacent coastal ranges, a valley, then a substantial mountain range as one moves inland. These are all good regions for first-class viticulture. By law, Catalonia is the only one of the three that does not enjoy the benefits of legitimate supplementary irrigation in the vineyard.

Of the 75,000ha suitable for agriculture in Penedès, one third or 25,000ha is planted to grapes. Other principal farming uses are cereals, olives and nuts - particularly hazel nuts.

When describing or considering land for viticulture, the French have a term that has become widely accepted as the best descriptor of grape growing needs - *terrior (*tair-wah):

Terroir has often been translated as *soil* or *earth* - and this is a very wrong definition. Terroir's true definition embraces soil certainly, but only as a minor part of the total equation. The major components are:

- the *slope* of the land. Catalonia enjoys a wide range of sloping and undulating land.

- *drainage* of the soil - free draining soils are desirable. Most Catalan soils are well drained.

- the *aspect* - does it face North, South, East or West to receive the maximum sun exposure? Most Penedès land has favoured aspects.

- is the vineyard at the *top, middle or bottom* of the slope. The *preferred* sites are nearly always in the middle of the slope.

- *frost* and *hail* probability - at anytime during the growing season frost and hail are public enemies number one in many countries. Both frosts and hail can be devastating in Penedès.

- *wind* - which can have enormous good — or bad — effects on vines. The good thing about cool breezes is that they keep the vine canopy cool and aired, so preventing disease. Strong winds actually do break the growing shoots causing loss of crops.

The year-long *Tramontana* wind is so famous in Ampurdán-Costa-Brava that the main street in Figueres is named for the beastly north wind. In this region, the Syrah grape will only grow in places that are entirely protected from the wind and other vines must be staked or trellissed to cope with its ferocity. This northern province is also savaged by other winds and locals will remind you of the sou' wester *Garbi* while others include the *Gregal, Llevant* and *Xaloc* Just one more hazard that grape growers face, no-one, anywhere is exempted from nature's disturbing ways in the vineyard.

Penedès has its *Mistral* wind which comes from the south then swings around to WNW or NW as the day grows. Speeds average 10-30 knots but gusts regularly exceed 50 knots. Yet, it is beneficial, as most winds are, in dispersing fungal diseases and avoiding them during the critical flowering season.

Through the gap in the coastal ranges near El Vendrell comes the *Marinada* a cooling breeze off the Mediterranean. It is quite cool in the mornings close to the coast then spreads through much of the Valley during the afternoon and evening. It is said by locals that this Mediterranean night moisture brings sufficient humidity so as to negate the necessity for supplementary irrigation. This is a difficult proposition to sustain.

Two photos from the same point at El Casots, Subirats, showing the landscape. Left photo looks across the Penedès Valley near Sant Sadurni d'Anoia to the western hills.

The right photo looking north to Barcelona shows the 9th century castle of Subirats with a modern day bodega in the foreground. Barcelona's industrial smog regularly obscures the Catalonian icon, Montserrat (serrated mountain) where the province's treasures were stored in the monastery during Spain's Civil war.

23

CLIMATE AND WEATHER

Climate is measured by long term averages. Climate determines which grape varieties will grow best in a given region — or even a specific site within a vineyard. Climate will also dictate whether the grapes will properly ripen - or not. *Weather is the day-to-day variation of those averages.* Weather helps to explain the particular characteristics of a given wine each year - and why it may be different (better or worse) than the "standard" for that appellation.

The best vintages occur when specific weather variables can be considered "normal" for the region.

Good wine can only be made in favourable climates and weather conditions. A good climate and poor weather will result in very little - if anything at all. Catalonia enjoys what is classified as a *Mediterranean* climate, the most agreeable of the five climate classifications for growing the generally preferred wine styles, particularly robust reds and full-bodied whites

The other four climate classifications are:

- *Continental* as found inland such as Catalonia's Lérida (Costers del Segre DO)
- *Marine West Coast* such as Oregon and Washington states in the USA, isolated regions of both Chile and Western Australia.
- *East Coast Hot* typified by Queensland (Australia), eastern China and southern North America.
- *East Coast Cold* is what the people experience in the states of New York and states further north.

Mediterranean climate can be found in many wine regions such as southern and western Australia, parts of California and Mexico, Chile,

South Africa and, obviously, those countries around the Mediterranean Sea. This climate's guidelines include long, hot, dry summers and mild winters when most rainfall is recorded. The benefits of Mediterranean climate are best illustrated by the difference between west and east coast wine areas of Australia, although the same applies in North and South American regions on either coast. The east coast regions have most rainfall in summer when the vines are growing and producing fruit. In some cases, the heaviest rain falls at harvest time which totally disrupts harvesting and reduces wine quality. These hot and humid summers attract fungal diseases which necessitate costly, defensive spray programs; usually applied weekly.

Mediterranean climates on the west (or south) coasts rarely have to spray for fungal diseases more than three times during the whole growing season. This in turn guarantees healthy, ripe fruit.

Like all other climates, Mediterranean climate is not faultless. When does it stop being Mediterranean and become *continental* climate as one moves further inland from the coast?

This is best defined by the length and severity of summer and winter seasons. Continental climates have withering hot summers and extremely cold winters with acute variation in seasons, normally less rainfall than their Mediterranean counterparts.

Catalonia, and parts of the Penedès DO, sit right on the Mediterranean. As one moves inland, even a short distance, it is the altitude.above sea level that changes the region's climate and weather patterns. The higher vineyards of Upper Penedès

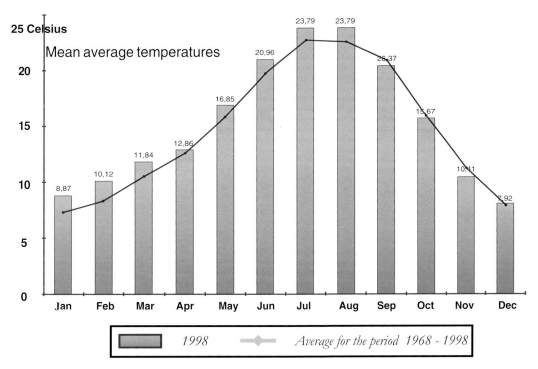

Mean average temperatures

25 Celsius

| | 1998 | Average for the period 1968 - 1998 |

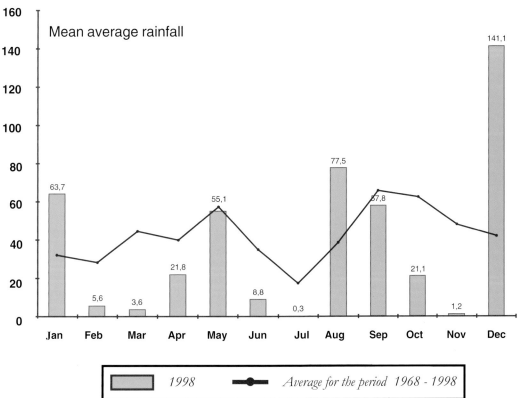

Mean average rainfall

| | 1998 | Average for the period 1968 - 1998 |

*The key elements to successful grapegrowing and, therefore, successful winemaking, are the right amount of sunshine and rain - at the **right** time. These averages over 30 years prove that Penedès has these two factors in the right proportions.*

are only 50 km from the coast but the altitude changes from zero to 800 metres (2,600 feet). This is an unusual and dramatic change of climate, weather and terroir and makes for very different wine styles.

Due to its wide variety of geographical conditions, Catalonia is a land of many climates.

On the northern border with France, the Pyrenees and their foothills have a typical mountain climate with winter temperatures below 0° C and annual rainfall of over 1,000 mm. There are heavy snowfalls in winter and the summers are relatively cool.

Throughout the Mediterranean coastal resorts of Costa Brava, Costa del Maresme, Barcelona, Costa del Garraf and Costa Daurada - and in the adjoining inland areas, the climate is pleasant and temperate. As a general rule, the further south one travels, the higher the temperatures and the lower the rainfall. Thus Girona has an annual rainfall of 800 mm as opposed to Tarragona's 525 mm; Penedès falls in between. There are also variations according to altitude. Expect about 1,000mm on the inland D'Ancosa mountain range, less on the coastal Garraf range.

The hinterland, far away from the sea, has a continental climate with cold winters and hot summers. Annual rainfall in the city of Lérida, Costre de Segre DO is 388 mm.

As illustrated on page 20, the three different regions of Penedès, although all Mediterranean climate, host different and fancied grape varieties. The Maritime route and the Penedès Valley are home to mainly the heat seeking grapes such as the local red and white varieties. The cooling significance of higher altitudes nurture the more northern European varieties. The region has the ability to produce quality wines of several distinct styles such as German Rieslings and the French Burgundy and Bordeaux styles in addition to their own local styles.

It is only in the last 20 years that two vintners recognised the benefits of this higher country to produce grapes eminently suited to international style wines. Jean Leon and Miguel A. Torres introduced this concept to Spain.

Although temperature is important it is only a small player in the overall picture. The black grapes which produce red wines need much higher temperatures for longer periods than white wine grapes, but, all grapes need sunshine directly onto the fruit. Grape bunches covered by shade in the heart of the canopy do not normally develop favourable varietal characters, direct sunshine alone does this. This recent finding has brought about a total re-think of the way grapes are grown and the ways they are managed in the vineyard - the buzz words are canopy management, pioneered by Australian guru, Richard Smart. who appears regularly on the Catalonia horizon.

Climate for winegrowing revolves around a simple axiom, the right amount of rain and sunshine *at the right time*. Catalan growers are blessed with sunshine aplenty. Rainfall and irrigation is another matter to be discussed elsewhere in the book. Yet, Catalan growers are handcuffed by laws about supplementary irrigation made by winegrowers in rain-abundant northern Europe. Only a fool would put a human being out in the hostile Spanish summer climate without drinking water. Why do these EEU officials think grape vines are any different to human beings as both have the same requirement for regular food and drink? Neither should be asked to suffer the whims of Mother Nature. Hopefully, we will see changes before many years pass.

However, if we look at the steady averages over the last 30 years on the page 25 charts, we can see both the good and bad of the Catalan climate. On average it is very good but, as everywhere else in the world, there are some devastating years. The very last one of the 20th century brought hail that devastated 2,000 ha of grapes at harvest time, a sad loss for those involved.

HELPFUL CATALAN/SPANISH WORDS

English	Catalan	Castilian Spanish
Amphitheatre type depression	Conca	Cuenca
Barrel	Bota	Barrica
Bottle	Ampolla	Botella
Cooperative	Cooperativa	Cooperativa
Cork	Suro/tap	Corcho/tapón
Corkscrew	Llevataps	Saca corchos
County	Comarca	Comarca
Earth/soil	Terra	Suelo/Tierra
Farm	Finca	Finca
Farmhouse	Mas/masia	Casa de campo
Food	Aliment/menjar	comida
Grape berry	Raïm	Racimo
Grape juice	Suc de raim	Jugo de uva
Hail	Pedra	Granizo/pedrisco
Harvest	Collita	Vendimia
Hill	Turo/serral	Colina
House	Can/casa	Casa
Label	Etiqueta	Etiqueta
Manager	Gerent	Gerente
Mountain range	Serralada	Cordillera
Mountainpeak	Cim/pic	Pico
Municipality	Municipi	Municipio
Must (wine)	Mosto	Mosto
Oak	Roure	Roble
Pruning	Poda	Poda
Rain	Pluja	Lluvia
River	Riu	Rio
State	l'Estat/provincia	El estado/provincia
Sun	Sol	Sol
Tank - stainless steel	Diposit d'acer inoxidable	Deposito de acer inoxidable
Tank - concrete	Diposit de címento	Depósit de cemento
Tasting	Tast	Degustacion
Tourist bureau	Oficina de Turisme	Oficina de Turismo
Train/railway	Ferrocarril	Tren/ferrocarril
Valley	Vall	Valle
Vine	Cep	Vidcepa
Vineyard	Vinyà	Viñedo
Viticulturist	Viticultor	Viticultor
Wind	Vent	Viento
Wine	Vi	Vino
Wine - red	Negre	Tinto
Wine - rosé	Rosat	Rosado
Wine - white	blanc	blanco
Winemaker	Enoleg	Enólogo
Winery	Celler/bodega	Bodega
Yeast	Llevat	Levadura

BOUNDARIES
POLITICAL, GEOGRAPHICAL & WINE

The Spanish and Catalan division of boundaries needs some explanation.

History has divided Spain according to the boundaries that once made-up the old kingdoms. As an outsider looking in, it is worth remembering that Spain is not a single, homogenous identity. Spain has four languages and five distinct identities. The languages are Basque, Castilian Spanish, Catalan and Galician. These languages are used (along with Castilian, which is spoken by all Spaniards) in the Basque Country, the central part of Spain, Catalonia and Galicia. Andalucia's identity is defined by its centuries-old association with Moorish rule. A long-time campaign for separatism which sometimes turned bloody, mainly by the Basques and Catalans, caused the national government in 1977 to divide the country into autonomous units, or *autonomias*, with considerable self-rule and financial control.

Catalonia has four provinces, Barcelona, Gerona, Lérida and Tarragona, each in turn divided into *comarcas* (counties) which are geographical areas - and still further down to *adjuntaments* (town councils) at the municipal level. For the sake of convenience, we will not go into political boundaries in this book. Rather, we will concentrate, where possible, on the divisions that define wine making areas.

Catalonia has nine distinct regions denominated as having their own (still) wine style and *terroir*. These are called *denominaciones de origen*, DOs for short. They are: Penedès (the largest and most important), Alella, Ampurdán-Costa Brava, Conca de Barberà, Pla de Bages, Costers del Segre, Terra Alta, Priorato and Tarragona.

Just to explain how complex the matter is, Penedès has three comarcas, that is, political - governmental divisions: Garraf which includes much of the coastal mountains and seaside resorts, Alt (Upper) Penedès covering most of the valley - and Baix (Lower) Penedès, which contains the southern most Mediterranean coastal part of the province. In terms of wine regions, Penedès also has three distinct areas, Baix or Lower Penedès, Mig or Middle Penedès and Alt or Upper Penedès. The difference, as you would expect, is each region's distance above sea level. However, these wine regions do not fit into the political regions bearing the same names. That is, the political Alt Penedès and the political Baix Penedès do not cover the same territory as their wine making namesakes. It is because of this confusion that we will try to a make things easier by using wine industry references rather than political ones.

No simplification is ever perfect, though. Sometimes you will find that a wine term does not quite fit into the geographical reality on the ground. For example, Torrelavit (a *municipi*) is an address used by wineries. If you look on a road map, however, the place does not seem to exist. The reason for this is that Torrelavit is actually a name resulting out of the geographical union of two growing towns, Lavit and Terrassola, but the road sign to both says Segura Viuda - a winery!

Urban pride by the residents of each town has meant that they have been loath to throw over their ancient names, which still appear on the maps, despite the fact that everyone knows their name is really Torrelavit. The *raison d'être* of this book is to make finding wineries and their best wines easy for you, so our maps will be as helpful as possible to the wine lover and the tourist who might be coaxed into expressing an interest in the wines of one of Europe's most picturesque and exciting wine regions.

REGULATING COUNCILS

Wine is one of mother nature's greatest gifts. What other beverage can tell you so much about the land from where it comes, the weather it encountered while growing as a plant and the people who made it? Before getting too romantic, however, it is wise to bear in mind that wine is also a food product, a basic form of nourishment over the centuries for many of the peoples of the Mediterranean. As such, rules and regulations apply to its growth and vinification, that is, the process used to turn it from fruit to wine.

In Spain, it is the European Union that governs broadly what insecticides, pesticides and herbicides can be used to protect the fruit. Further down, the Spanish government has the right and the obligation to ensure that foodstuffs worthy of human consumption reach the dinner tables of its citizens. Wine is such a noble product, though, with its own antiseptic agent already built in (alcohol), that many of these regulations are simple, fail-safe positions. Nevertheless, great care is taken to ensure that what a wine advertises on its label is the truth.

What may be more difficult for the wine tourist to understand, is the nature of the *Denominaciones de Origen*, and of the *Consejos Reguladores* that govern them. These are terms you will see on most bottles sold in Catalonia. Denominación de Origen is a title granted to a wine growing region that, following years, and is some cases centuries, of observation can be said to have its own character, style and terroir. Traditionally, you should be able to identify wines, tasting them blind, by their distinctive regional character. The Consejos Reguladores were set up, to begin with by conscientious growers themselves, to see that the quality and character of these styles was not unduly tampered with. Above them sits the overall governmental body, called the *Subdirección General de Vinos de Calidad* to oversee that mini-

mum standards are adhered to. Initially there were benefits for both grower and consumer. As word of mouth information spread that a wine from a certain DO was really worth buying, and that its quality could be relied upon because it varied very little, prices went up and were maintained within predictable parameters. To many growers it made sense to belong to such an organisation as it more or less guaranteed a reliable income for their efforts. Styles became more refined as growers found that certain grape varieties and vinification techniques added depth and meaning to the regional characteristics of their wines.

Eventually, wines from each denominated region grew to be as typical of that region as the cuisine they complemented. It is worth remembering that the term denominación de origen applies just as rigorously to some olive oils and cheeses as it does to wines, in an effort to maintain their distinctiveness in the marketplace.

The trouble with this system, when applied to wine, is that modern technology, that began to revolutionise the Spanish wine industry as of the late 1960s, has radically altered the tastes of the wines that used to be so typical of the regions of Spain. A well made Tempranillo from one region may now taste not too dissimilar from an equally well made Tempranillo from the opposite corner of the country, not to mention one produced in Argentina, Australia or Chile.

Although it is understandable that some regions, like Jerez (that makes Sherry) and Rioja, should try to protect the essential character of a product that is virtually unique and has achieved world status, it begins to make less sense when considering modern winemaking globally. One can still see some of the attraction of the DO system, but at the same time it is worth keeping an eye on world-wide competition. There is a lot of magic and beauty in wine, but there is also the need to make money and to keep Spain's rural workforce employed. Winemakers in Australia and Chile value outright quality far more than regional typicity, and European consumers, seem to agree with this *modus operandi*.

Before the advent of the EEU (European Common Market Union) each country ran their own regulations which were surprisingly consistent in that everybody paid lip-service to the status quo. Now, everything is controlled by Brussels so there is but one standard for all members of the Common Market. The Brussels bureaucrats regard the highest wine standard as V.C.P.R.D., (*vino de calidàd producido en región determinàda*) or broken down to the individual nations as *appellation control* (AO) or, in the case of Spain, *Denominacion de Origin* (DO). Another classification outside the DO rating is *vino de la tiera* or wines of the earth/soil, a classification that demands a vintage date and variety.

Vino de mesa (table wines) are outside these regulations and can reflect anything from supreme excellence to downright terrible, the price will usually reflect the quality. These wines do not need a vintage date or place of origin.

It is worth commenting that DO standards are anything but consistent from one DO to another, something like a ping pong ball in an ocean storm. They vary enormously from wave to wave - there is no standard. Even worse, all judges are incestuously drawn from the local community.

There are, of course, exceptions. Some wineries have established reputations for producing high quality wine, sometimes as a brand, and prefer to buy the wines or grapes from where ever in Spain they choose, so as to guarantee quality. Despite the fact that these wines, often careful blends, have to be sold as vino de mesa, their fame is such that prices remain high. Nevertheless, most winemakers in Spain prefer to go the well-trodden route, and seek to sell their wines as DO wines. Spanish consumers also seem to prefer the *status quo* because the consumption of DO wines has risen sharply, while that of vino de mesa has dropped dramatically.

The type of wine made within a denominated region is the decision of its regulating council. Some Consejos Reguladores are more forward thinking than others. Today in Penedès the Consejo Regulador is composed as follows. There are 5,800 *viticultores*, or grape growers in the region and 138 *cellers*, or wineries. Each has the right to say how things should be governed. As these numbers would make for a very unwieldy organisation, matters are simplified. Viticultores elect six of their colleagues to the Council, and wineries also elect six of their peers to sit on the Council. These twelve councillors then appoint a president to the regulating council of the Denominación de Origen Penedès. Decisions are taken democratically.

Wines made within the denominated region have to be deemed as stylistically typical and of sufficient quality to merit the right to sport the DOs name on the label. This is determined by panels that judge the wines "blind" and also by laboratory analysis that ensure no undue process has been used in making the wine. When a wine is first made, four samples are set to one side, one for analysis, one for evaluation, one as back-up at the bodega and a spare held at the offices of the Consejo Regulador, should a dispute arise. All bottles are sealed at the same time, with the same seal, to ensure fairness.

Some major producers in the region, such as Miguel Torres, have, on occasion, found it frustrating to operate exclusively within the bounds of the DO Penedès. These frustrations were first triggered from abroad, when a European Council resolution determined that in future DOs should take legal precedence on wine labels over brand names and trade marks, regardless of antiquity. So, Torres Vedras (a DO in Portugal) could make exclusive use of the word 'Torres' on labels. Imagine Miguel Torres's reaction when he was informed that the use of his ancestral name on his wine labels was to become illegal in Europe!

CATALAN LABEL LANGUAGE

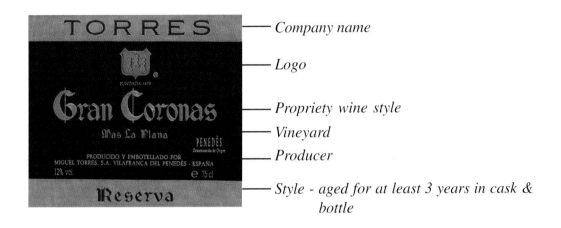

— Company name

— Logo

— Propriety wine style

— Vineyard

— Producer

— Style - aged for at least 3 years in cask & bottle

Fermented in barrel —

Capacity & alcohol content —

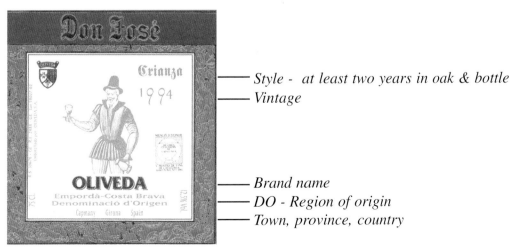

— Style - at least two years in oak & bottle

— Vintage

— Brand name

— DO - Region of origin

— Town, province, country

The Grapes

On Being A Grape

Red wines are made from red, purple and black grapes, these are referred to as black grapes. Rosé or Rosada wines, very important in Europe, are also made from black grapes. Of course, "white" grapes and wines aren't really white, but varying degrees of green to pink, including the entire yellow range.

As if the winelover needs any more terrorizing from an industry that thrives on intimidation, almost every grape has a plurality of names. This was fine in the days when horses and canoes were the main means of transportation and nobody had a clue what was happening 100km away. In these days of jet transportation and electronic media this ridiculous situation has to be resolved sooner or later; the sooner the better.

Due to the uniqueness of numerous Catalan and Spanish grapes, this nomenclature multiplicity (called synonyms) has caused considerable problems ensuring accuracy in this section of the book. The study of grapes is known as ampelography and, historically, most of the published literature has emanated from France. Even though the French give their own names to grapes, a list of synonyms for each variety is usually listed. These French scholars irregularly tour the world updating their information and checking new varieties and clones.

Even though a grape may have a 2,000 year history in Spain, that grape will be listed in the text books under its French name. Here's where the tug-of-war commences. The French/Spanish border, which includes Catalonia, is a very productive winegrowing area and its here and other places that the same grape can have three different names, bearing in mind that the French people in this corner speak Catalan as well - and the Spanish citizens speak Catalan and Spanish. Another problem is that a Spanish vineyard may cross the French border several times.

So the popular Spanish variety Mourvedre, is called just that on the France side, Monastrell or Mataro on the Spanish side. Then every province or department in Spain and France that grows the grape has traditionally given the vine a name of their own choosing, names describing the growth habit of the vine such as upright growth or heavy bloom on the grape berry. The common names Mataro and Mourvedre are the towns who claim place of the grape's origin. Mataro is a fast growing city just north of Barcelona while Mourvedre is adapted from the town of Murviedro in Valencia.

A problem then arises when an normally competent author publishes a definitive work claiming that Monastrell and Mourvedre are different varieties while another even more competent professional ampelographer does not acknowledge the Monastrell synonym, nor mention it at all, a slap in the eye for a grape that is planted on 100,000 ha (247,000 acres) in Spain! After considerable research, we are happy to report that they are one and the same thing.

A similar problem exists with many grapes which makes for mammoth confusion among consumers. A sterile wine media refuses to take a lead in educating consumers or browbeating the industry into some standard nomenclature. For 25 years this author has asked scientific bodies in several countries to accept a standard set of grape names but everyone has an isolationist attitude; incredible in this day and age. By way of example, in the relatively short distance from Andalusia to Marseilles one text book lists 27, yes 27, synonyms for the variety Monastrell or

Mourvdre! Will we ever learn?

The natural pigment in blue or black grape skins is chemically identical to the pigment in red wine. Chemistry within the cell structure of grape skins causes the same pigment to appear blue, purple or black in the berry's skin, but mainly red or crimson in the juice or wine.

Size of the grape berries can be indicative of wine quality. As an example, some of the best varieties, such as Cabernet Sauvignon, Pinot noir, Riesling and (Gewurz)Traminer, have small berries on small clusters. Also, there are several distinctive berry shapes; however, no relationship between berry shape and wine quality has been suggested to date.

Grape cluster/bunch shapes are described as *cylindrical, conical, winged or shouldered* and berry closeness to each other as, *loose, well-filled or compact,* but the shape is used more to help identify varieties than to predict wine quality. Nevertheless, these differences become quite important when the weather turns bad before harvest — tight clusters being far more susceptible to mildew and rot than loose, easy drying clusters. Local weather conditions, particularly, frost, wind and rain, will be the main determinant in which varieties are planted in a given region.

Although there are thousands of grape varieties, only a few hundred are cultivated for winemaking, their origins being a study in geography. Over the centuries each winegrowing region in Europe sorted out the different varieties that had been left by the conquerors, keeping only those few which found local favor. This is a problem faced by New World vignerons, they are still learning which varieties are best suited to their own particular region.

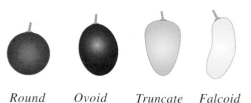

Round   *Ovoid*   *Truncate*   *Falcoid*

Syrah - cylindrical, well-filled

Macabeo - winged, compact

Monastrell - shouldered, very compact

Garnacha - conical, loose

Past, Present & Future

Over the centuries, Penedès and Catalonia, like other European regions, have selected their own unique grape varieties from the vast number of odd varieties brought to the their country by the Greeks, Romans, Carthaginians - and explorers even before them. While many varieties from other countries and regions have found a home in the New World, the white grapes and some red varieties of Catalonia have stayed at home.

(It is worth noting here that all grapes in the Southern Hemisphere came south with the European settlers. There are no indigenous grapes on any of the southern continents.)

It is reasonable to ponder that for some years yet, Catalonia's major wine markets will be at home and local varieties will satisfy that market. They are relatively easy and economical to produce. With more specialization and application *Parellada* and *Xar-relo* can be developed into very good varieties - but, never world-beaters. However a media driven world is global and the demand is for Chardonnay - a variety popping-up all over Catalonia. Some of these new wines are very good, a lot very ordinary and there some pathetic examples of this noble variety.

Our thoughts are that this Chardonization is a major mistake, a me-too situation; you can make it, so can I. As the 20th century closed, the four corners of the world were glutted with Chardonnay. We believe that consumers in the first decade of the new millennium will be looking for new and different flavours.

The white grapes that can be grown to provide the flavours of the future are Viognier, Chenin (blanc) and Verdelho; these are ideally suited to Catalonian regions. Maybe Marsanne, another Rhone variety like Viognier, is also a potential star. All four varieties are successful in similar Australian climates and this is a very important indicator for Catalonia. These varieties would certainly offer the international oenophile some relief from the flood of the dreaded Chardonnay and Sauvignon (blanc) wines.

It is fair to say that today's consumer is better educated, and more discriminating, than ever before. It is a folly to think that these affluent afficionados will suffer the worn-out flavours of the last century. The same applies to the current wave of Cabernet and Merlot mania. A new world of free-thinkers will be looking for Cariñena, Tempranillo, Garnacha (Grenache elsewhere) and their blends; wines with real flavour without a lifetime of waiting..

Catalonia is already a proven red wine producers dream. We believe that Catalonia is not even at the beginning of its greatness, they have only been through the warm-up events to prove a theory. It is easy to name the people in most regions who have caste the stamp of greatness, a mould that is relatively easy to follow. Whether it be with Cabernet Sauvignon, Garnacha, Merlot, Pinot noir, Tempranillo, Catalan producers from a number of regions have, for the last decade, made a positive statement that the future is here - now! Yet, there is much to do in the vineyards, new/old red wine varieties with broader appeal such as Syrah, Monastrell and the Portuguese Tintos have a very definite place in Catalonia's future.

Catalonia's wine schools are on track; graduating students are better trained and have an extroverted global vision. Each year the number of quality wines increases from more regions; it is a band waggon that everyone knows they must join. Come visit us and be part of a new history, as many of these fabulous wines can only be found on the wine routes of Catalonia!

THE LOCAL STARS

At this time white grapes dominate Catalonia vineyard plantings, due mainly to the world-wide demand for the famous *cava* (sparkling) wines; the world's two largest sparkling wine producers are located in Penedès.

Three local grapes essential in producing the region's fabulous sparkling varieties, Macabeo (mack-a-bay-oh), Xarel-lo (cha-rel-lo) and Parellada (Parell-ah-dah). Fortunately, these grapes have also been widely adapted locally for still table wines.

It is of interest that each of these varieties grow in their own particular region. Macabeo can be found mainly, but not exclusively, in the Maritme Penedès areas near the coast,. Xarel-lo dominates in the Penedès Valley region, while Parellada (pictured here) does best in the cooler regions on the mountain slopes. Of course, this is a broad generalization.

These varieties are used for both varietal and blended wines - the blended wines being very definitely for early consumption - the joven wines so popular as everyday beverage wines. How the varietals will fare in the market place over the next few years of export penetration into other countries, particularly Europe, will be an interesting exercise.(See Wine Styles page 45). Some producers such as Albet i Noya are devoting the appropriate amount of effort and time to realise the full potential of the Penedès white grapes. More effort by more people in developing these grapes will surely benefit everyone. For so long, the whole subject of these three local white grapes has been solely focussed on their use in cava. We have enjoyed a number of stimulating discussions with local identities about the white wine future and potential of these grapes.

The three major red varieties Garnacha tinto, better known as Grenache in many places, Tempranillo and Cariñena, are now common in forward-thinking, red wine producing countries around the world. While all three are made as superb varietal wines, many producers will choose to use them as a component of blended reds. Some Australian producers, notably d'Arenberg in Mc Laren Vale, have been winning gold medals and trophies for more than a quarter of a century with an outstanding Grenache-Syrah pressings blend. This is a style that could well be adopted in Catalonia.

As noted on ensuing pages, Garnacha is an outstanding partner for many reds wines including Cabernet Sauvignon, Tempranillo, Monastrell and Garnacha/Cabernet blends produces exquisitely, high-priced wines from Priorato that the author cannot afford! Other varieties such as Syrah are also finding their way into these famous blends. The Tempranillo/Cabernet blend is also made with distinction in several other Spanish regions.

Parellada

GARNACHA TINTO

For far too long, far too many people, who know far too little, with self-styled titles — have gone from one London UK wine event to another, bad-mouthing Garnacha as being a blending-only wine; what incredible ignorance of today's world.

If one could have a love affair with grapes, few people would select the same as this writer - Garnacha tinto - red, (there is also a Garnacha blanc - white), Pinot noir, Syrah and Viognier. To me, they are the spice of life, at the price of an affordable romance.

What is so appealing about Garnacha, Spain's most widely planted red wine grape? Firstly, it is a very good all-rounder making excellent Rosé's, red wines of wide ranging styles, an excellent blending wine with many other varieties, and, a flirtatious, bosomy lady when out on her own. As many aficionados know, as Grenache it is the foundation of France's Chateauneuf de Pape wines, being one of the 13 permissible grapes in that region. Garnacha also produces superb sweet wines when fortified in the light Port style.

Wine should taste as though it was made from grapes — and despite rough handling on many occasions, Garnacha always comes through with lots of fruit; luscious berry fruit. As with Pinot noir, Garnacha also has *sweet* fruit, even though the wine will have no residual sugar at all. Usually it has the same velvety smoothness in the mouth as Pinot noir; a trait I find appealing, particularly with food. None of that Cabernet, barbed-wire tannin needing eons to be tamed, for this writer. After all, Sauvignon is synonymous with savage. Yet when these grapes are blended into a single wine, the result is something that would satisfy the most ardent Bordeaux lover.

Garnacha is tough in hot, dry and windy climates. On the down side Garnacha can suffer *downy mildew* problems at flowering time thus re-ducing the potential crop. In the winery it is prone to oxidation and requires attention to detail; so what?

Fortunately, Garnacha has thinner skins than the tannic monster Cabernet — and if over-cropped will yield innocuous juice. Sadly this has been its past in most places. However, a more informed world is coming to grips with this reality, and realizes that Garnacha is the only grape to plant on hot, windy, infertile hilltops. Garnacha is yield sensitive. Highly fertile soils, and abundant rainfall seasons, will produce very pumped-up, ordinary wines.

Garnacha is capable of producing world-class wines in Australia, California, Greece, Lebanon, Sardinia and other Mediterranean regions. In fact, in a recent London UK wine magazine judgement of a large number of Garnacha wines from around the world (by an all British panel), a Sardinian wine topped the event, Australian wines took 16 of the first 20 places, France two places and Spain only one. The Australian wines all came from South Australia; the driest state on earth's driest continent.

What does this mean? To this author, it means that Catalonia has not yet discovered its own jewel, while at the same time searching for jewels in other places. Wine producers in the Romantic nations have found the discipline of severe summer pruning rather distasteful; throwing away potentially good grapes is tough medicine. But, a vine is a sports car, not a giant truck capable of carrying heavy loads. Each and every vine must be fine-tuned, if it is to produce good fruit for world class wine.

Only where this discipline is rigorously instituted will Garnacha find its rightful place among the great wines of the world.

MONASTRELL

TEMPRANILLO

It is hard imagine a grape variety named "dog-strangler" or estrangle-chien in the French. That is but one of the many synonyms given to the variety Monastrell, known in other places as Mourvedre and Mataro. Monastrell was handed the strangler handle due to the hard, astringent flavour of the grape. Amazing that someone has not called Cabernet Sauvignon the elephant-strangler?

The astringent characters of Monastrell come from medium sized, conical and winged bunches of compact, small berries which are high in tannin and extract. The berries are almost white with a heavy covering of *bloom*. What does the above mean? Simply, it means that there is a low juice to skin ratio which gives the wine more tannin and skin extracts including colour. Tempranillo also has it, Garnacha does not. Once the berry skin is broken the *bloom* contains sufficient wild yeast's to start the fermentation process as the sweet juice contacts the yeast.

Only in the last decade have some courageous Spanish vintners brought a varietal Monastrell to the market. As with several other Spanish varieties, they all need some avante garde New World experimentation to show what can be done with these neglected grapes. Certainly a grape variety for the winelover to watch with interest.

Garnacha

Monastrell

If there is one problem with the Catalan language it is that grapes are given a distinctly local name as opposed to Spanish or other European names. In Catalonia, Tempranillo (pronounced temp-prah-nee-yoh) is called Ull de Llebre (eye of the jack-rabbit), while in southern Spain it is known as Cencibel. What the world, let alone Catalonia, needs is more confusing grape synonyms and useless names. Leave that to the Australians; they have refined useless names to an art form.

While Garnacha maybe the true-blue Spanish grape and the most widely planted, Tempranillo is the muscular grape that has the features of the popular Bordeaux tannic types. Temprano is Spanish speak for early - so this grape probably received its name because it is the earliest of the black grapes harvested. This usually happens towards late September whereas Garnacha is picked mid-late October.

Tempranillo

Despite the relatively low acid content, the structure of Tempranillo wine is much more upright in the mouth than Garnacha which generally has a lovely soft round feeling. The classic, as opposed to the popular, wine styles coming from Tempranillo, usually with a healthy dose of another variety, are for collectors and investors rather than the take home and drink style. Yet, there are far more joven (young) styles than the classic firm types.

Tempranillo rewards the drinker with an abundance of plum and cherry flavours. When blended with small amounts of Monastrell and/ or Cabernet, Tempranillo can seduce the most ardent claret lover.

OTHER LOCAL VARIETIES

CARIÑENYA: Here is another of those vinous conundrums. A Spanish grape variety by birth but adopted by the Mediterranean regions of France where it is a major producer, far more so than in its native Spain. The French know it as Carignan, obviously the Italians affixed an o to the end to make it Carignano, and the Australians and Californians don't really care how it is spelt.

Due to the vines tenacious hold in the ground, if one does not like the variety Carineña is difficult to eliminate. It favours hot climates but also loves every disease that can affect a grape vine thereby demanding copious sprays. In return it gives bountiful yields of juice high in acid, colour, tannins and alcohol. Yet, not until blending with more flavourful varieties such as Garnacha does it become anything exciting to talk about. Carineña has been a wonderful source of cheap wine for those around the Mediterranean who have a fondness for their everyday plonk.

The truth about Carineña is its capability of making truly great wine when blended with the right components. One only has to see some super-Catalan wines, Torres Grans Muralles for example, to see what stunning heights this denigrated grape can reach. Excellent quality wines made from Carineña can be found almost anywhere from Tarragona to the Costa Brava. Have a serious look at the wines of Oliveda in Capmany, Ampurdán.

MACABEO: Of Catalonia's own three white grapes, Macabeo, known in Catalonia as Macabeu - elsewhere as Viura, is the most prolific and has the most compact bunches of the three cava grapes. No one seriously suggests that it will be a star in its own right, but may win an Oscar for best supporting actor in the world of cava.

As it is believed to have strong roots in the Middle East, Macabeo was probably brought to Spain by the Moors and it is this heat-loving background that makes it a favourite in the low, warm Mediterranean Penedés. Flavourwise, Macabeo is a fairly neutral, if slightly floral, variety which appeals to the cava producers. When grown in the cooler regions of the Pyrenees it can develop some good qualities.

Macabeo has the virtue of being a late budding variety, much later than Chardonnay, and is not Spring frost prone. However, as Macabeo is subject to bunch rot (botrytis) it must be harvested early, at low alcohol and relatively high acid levels. Hence it produces very crisp, fresh wines in the 11% alcohol range. In Penedés, its future is important, albeit in blended joven and cava wines.

PARELLADA: A most engaging bunch with its loose, attractively coloured berries. Parellada has a big following for its potential as a first-class table wine when grown in the cool climates of the higher Penedés region. All three cava grapes are conical, Parellada has well-filled, almost compact bunches with tough skins making it less inclined to botrytis. It susceptible to dry seasons yet continues regularly to yield fine grapes making aromatic wines relatively low (10-11%) in alcohol. In a table wine sense, the best is yet to come from this variety; certainly worth watching..

XAREL-LO: Despite their affinity as partners in cava, Xarel-lo is almost the opposite of Macabeo. The buds burst early making it susceptible to loss and damage through late Spring frosts. Xarel-lo has strong vegetal flavors and relatively high alcohol levels which some producers believe they can tame. It is drought resistant and less prone to botrytis. Along with Macabeo and Parellada it is an ideal component of cava and the joven whites at about 11% alcohol.

However, it should not be lightly dismissed. As with its sister Parellada, Xarel-lo should be given a full trial in the hands of non-traditional, avant-garde oenologists from Catalonia and other countries. Considered to be a variety with a future in table wine production. A definite Spanish flavour.

GARNACHA BLANCA: The white mutation of Garnacha Noir, and a major contributor in Catalan areas outside of Penedés. Here is yet another Spanish variety that needs a working over by the avant-garde oenologist. The grape has good flavour and provides higher levels of alcohol than the three cava sisters. One commentator suggests that it can be a parallel to Marsanne, a sound that rings nicely for lovers of this Rhone variety. One can only believe that Marsanne would do extremely well in selected Catalan regions. Garnacha blanca is a more mouth-filling wine than the cava sisters and has appeal through lower acidity which can, if necessary, be adjusted in the bodega.

FUTURE VARIETIES: Just as the dawning of the 20th century brought a host of changes in fashions and flavours, our new century will bring with it desires for new and different flavours. A burgeoning place like Catalonia, full of promise and hope will be able to provide this demand. Other than Marsanne mentioned above, the Portuguese variety Verdelho which has proven itself for more than half a century in the equally dry and harsh climate of Western Australia, should be at the top of any shopping list.

FOREIGN VARIETIES

Chardonnay: Chardonnay is the source of France's white Burgundy wines, as well as fine sparkling and table wines around the world. It has a wide climatic tolerance and is known for good to exceptional quality when grown in almost any climatic region.

The vine is vigorous and easy to farm except for a susceptibility to mildew, bunch rot and botrytis. Because the buds push out early in spring, Chardonnay vines are subject to spring frost damage.

The small to medium size, well-filled bunches and berries yield an amazing diplay of flavours that are dominated by the region in which they are grown. Cool climates produce flavours of green apple, lemon/lime citrus acidity, fresh pineapple, melon, fig, floral and many others. Grapes grown in warmer climates will yield wonderful aromas and flavours of tropical fruits, fresh stone fruits such as apricots, peaches and nectarines, and also canned pineapple and stone fruits.

Chenin (blanc): A leading variety in France's Loire region, California's Central Valley, Australia and South Africa where it is the most prolific white variety. Grown in the right regions, Chenin can be a truly wonderful variety, even carrying modest amounts of barrel fermentation and ageing to advantage. Chenin should be on the Catalan drawing board for many good reasons including its ability to provide flavoursome wines of good acidity in a hot climate.

Bunches are medium-large in size, winged or even double, conical and compact. Berries are juicy and tough-skinned. Fully ripe, flavoursome Chenin responds well to limited time in barrels. It is considered a good blending variety, the flavours which include apple, lemon and pineapple are compatible with a large number of more distinctive varieties, from Chardonnay to Semillon.

Riesling: This is Germany's most important grape, but it is also cultivated in most of the world's coolest vineyard climates. Widely grown in northern and eastern Europe. Fruit is susceptible to sunburn which can cause skin and juice browning and destroy the varietal flavor.

Appearance of the fruit is "white," as if covered by a white powder. Striking and different from that of all other wine grapes. In cooler vineyards this variety produces delicate, flowery and perfumy wines of great distinction. Wines are mostly dry but semi-sweet styles are popular.

Sauvignon (blanc): This variety is known for its use in the dry wines of the regions near Bordeaux, France.

In New Zealand, where the varietal flavor is cultivated to its most emphatic levels, is probably the world leader in this variety. The natural flavor is intensely flavoursome and in very cool climates it becomes minty or lime-like and pungent.

The clusters are small and compact, but often winged shape — a characteristic usually found in larger clustered varieties that ripen relatively early. Berries are a definite greenish color, small and oval. Skins are thin and the variety is easily susceptible to *botrytis cinerea,* or noble rot; even where humidity isn't high.

Flavours vary from gooseberry through herbaceous and include lime, lemon, grassy, melon,

Traminer (*Gewurz*): One of the earliest ripening varieties, this "Germanic" grape (from the Italian village of Tramin) thrives in cool climates. Even so, it is often planted in medium-warm regions, presumably because of its unusually "spicy, flowery" flavor. Gewurz is the German word for spicy; yet not all Traminer vines are the spicy variety.

Although considered a white grape, Traminer fruit is noticeably pink in color. The wines are never pink or red as concentration of pigment in the skins is inconsequential. The vine is not vigorous although it is fairly resistant to vineyard diseases. Skins are tough and yields are moderate. Absolutely ideal accompaniment to many Chinese dishes.

Cabernet Sauvignon: Some claim this is the only grape allowed in Heaven! Cabernet Sauvignon is one of the premium red wine grape in Argentina, Australia, Bordeaux, California, Chile, and South Africa. Its wines are known for pronounced flavor, color, body, acidity and longevity. Sadly, the media driven Cabernet fervor has caused many winelovers to overlook a number of equally pleasurable wines of exquisite flavor such as Barbera, Nebbiolo, Pinot noir, Sangiovese, Syrah, Tempranillo and Zinfandel. However, for some years now Catalan Cabernets have beaten the world's best, even the top French wines - in Paris!

Best in warm climates, Cabernet has produced very good wines in other regions, even Germany! The tough skin and loose cluster help make this grape very resistant to mildew, bunch rot, botrytis and other diseases. Fully mature grapes are blue in color due to a gray bloom covering the surface of the heavily pigmented skins. The vines are easy to work with, producing well (up to 11 tons per hectare) and requiring no special care in vineyards. The Cabernets are also "winemakers" wines, fermenting smoothly, handling well and ageing beautifully in oak barrels and in bottle.

Cabernet Franc: Being a close relative of Cabernet Sauvignon, this variety is a Bordeaux, France, native. Often blended with Merlot (in Pomerol and St. Emilion) and Cabernet Sauvignon (in many areas) to produce highly regarded red wines. The varietal aroma is reminiscent of raspberries and, sometimes, violets.

Similar to Cabernet Sauvignon in growth habits and ease of handling, the vigor is good and yield is productive. However, it is more sensitive than Cabernet Sauvignon to mildew

Merlot: Merlot produces soft, perfumed wines which are often blended with Cabernet in France and in many New World countries. Unblended, produces outstanding wines in the St. Emilion and Pomerol areas of France as well as in Italy, Switzerland and California. It is one of the few European vines to succeed in Japan. South America has large plantings as have most other wine growing regions the world over. Merlot has adapted well to Penedés conditions and has a strong presence in many top class reds. Flavours include cherry, plum, tobacco, licorice & toffee.

Pinot noir: When well made in the right climatic years, Pinot noir, arguably, reaches heights not attained by other varieties. Aptly called a "minx", Pinot noir makes the highest classification of (red) wines in Burgundy as well as methode traditionale sparkling wines right around the world. It is most suited to cool climates and is extensively planted in Switzerland, northern Italy and even Germany (where it is called Spatburgunder).

Pinot noir is not easy to grow and many consider it is difficult to handle in the cellar, simply because it cannot be handled in the same manner as other red wines with thicker skins. Compact bunches and thin skins make it vulnerable to almost any vineyard diseases. With the best clones, correct vineyard locations and dedicated vignerons, Pinot noir very definitely has a place in Catalonia. The flavours of good Pinot are magic!

Syrah: Called both Shiraz and Hermitage in Australia, this Rhone variety produces a robust wine with ample color, fruit and tannin. Syrah is blended with as many as a dozen other varieties to produce the wines of Chateauneuf-du-Pape in France. It is an important variety in the small Priorato region and also Ampurdán. However, the strong Catalan winds will always present a problem. The variety responds strongly to the climate of a growing region; wine quality may vary markedly from one vineyard to another

Posing as Shiraz, this grape has performed splendidly in Australia for more than 150 years where it is successful in both warm and cool areas. Syrah is used alone or blended with Cabernet Sauvignon to produce complexity, fullness and early drinkability. Good Syrah is like a mouthfull of berries, include any red berry you can think of from blue to black. In cool climates it exhibits an intense peppery flavour. Do not confuse it with the Petite Sirah of California.

Women in Wine!

Eva Refecas
Oenologist, Mas Tinell

Maria Galup Tormé
Oenologist, Covides

Mireya Torres
Oenologist, Miguel Torres

Joaña Viñas
Oenologist, J. M. Raventos

Maite Esteve i Julia
Manager, Vins El Cep

WINE STYLES

Wine styles, like art or music, vary with the consumers likes and dislikes, socio-economic status, nationality and even religion. Those considered the "best" - whatever that is - customarily come from some regions of France - Bordeaux and Burgundy in particular, and from Germany. Predictably they are outrageously expensive, yet they represent less than five percent of all wines produced. Many are purchased by investors who feed the interminable wine auctions.

It is said that 80 percent of all wine is consumed within 24 hours of purchase so one could argue that this is the world's dominant style of wine. One might fairly ask, "and, what is that style?" This "popular" style would include packaged bulk wine in cardboard casks, 1500mL bottles and other large bottles, and what are known as the "fighting varietals" — low-priced 750mL bottles of popular varietal wines such as Chardonnay, Sauvignon, Merlot and Cabernet.

These dominant style wines are extremely good value-for-money. Invariably fruity, they will rarely benefit from ageing; they are made to be consumed soon after purchase. In most cases this means the same year as the wine is made. In all probability the grapes will come from irrigated, desert/arid-type climates such as Australia's Murray and Murrumbidgee River regions, California's central desert, Argentina's Mendoza and San Juan areas or South Africa inland areas, which all use supplementary irrigation to assure abundant crops.

By law European producers have not been able to use irrigation (this is changing), so they have had access only to what nature provides. Therefore the high producing regions, from Spain to Greece, are those close to the Mediterranean with assured rainfall. As one moves away from the coast, rainfall drops dramatically.

Every wine producer wants to create his/her own scenario - whether it be soil, climate, grape variety, tradition, technology or whatever. The reason is simple, that's all they have - and that is how the laws of wine production operate throughout the world. A perfect example is the small region of France's Burgundy where five grapes are permissible, yet only two bring the volume of returns - Chardonnay and Pinot noir. From the southern Maconaisse to the "golden slopes" in the north, prices increase up to 10 times as the winelover moves north. Can the wines possibly be ten times better?

Old established and relatively small French regions such as Burgundy, Chablis, Champagne and to a lesser extent Bordeaux, have all worked to create an unsubstantiated myth that they have the "tablets of stone" when it comes to wine quality and style. While they may have been the benchmark for their particular style within each region, the mythical quality of supposed excellence, can vary ten fold. The whole scenario is driven by images (the prevaricator of the early 21st century) and shortages of highly publicised, as opposed to high quality products.

It is a strange phenomenon that nearly all these supposedly benchmark products take years - even up to 20 years - to reach drinkability whereas the 80 percent of wines consumed each day reach that stage in one year. This surely defies logic?

Because the above wines are benchmarks, blindly followed by producers around the world, any dissimilar products are considered to be "different" i.e. not good - whatever "not good" means? To quote the late Prof. Maynard Amerine, arguably the scientific father of the New World wine revolution, "California makes the best California wines in the world!" This is the author's hypothesis for Catalan wines - they are the best Catalan wines in the world. However, many are different - even if a top Catalan Cabernet has bested the best of France, according to French judges — and what's more - in gay Paris! This was also achieved with a Torres Chardonnay.

To compete in these never-ending international wine judgings it is preferable for producers to make a so-called *international* wine, a style based on the European benchmarks. This is being done more and more in the New World to cater for the large export markets in the UK, USA, Japan and northern European, especially Scandanavian, countries. This is also the thrust of the export-oriented Catalan producers.

Spain has a number of wine classifications of wines including *vino de mesa* table wine*, vino comarcal* (wine of the comarca)*, vino de la tierra* (country wine), *joven, crianza, reserva* and *gran reserva*. We will deal mainly with the last four categories.

Joven (young) wine represents the biggest portion of quality wine; take it home and drink it! With crianza wines we are moving to the first step of the serious "talking" wines.

Crianza is the first level of aged wines - with or without oak barrel ageing; without being very uncommon. Crianza requires a minimum of two years ageing, normally six months in oak. It is not uncommon for crianza wines to be held for more than the two years mandatory maturation period. Then they start moving towards the reserva category which demands three years maturation with at least one year in oak and another in bottle.

Gran reserva wines are only made in the best vintage years. These are the winery's flag ship wine with a minimum of two years in cask and a total of five years in the cellar before release.

The USA wine trade has adopted a ridiculous classification for bottled wine starting with *premium* which one would think was the best. Wrong, it's the lowest category and is followed by *super premium* and *ultra-premium*! For a long time Britons have classified some wines as being *fine* wines - whatever shade of grey that is? Maybe it is a guide to those strange people who invest in wine - rather than enjoy drinking this liquid gold.

If these nebulous adjectives can be eliminated and we assume that our long-nosed, wine adventurer desires to gauge the style of wine made in the ten Catalonia DOs, the fact is that Catalonia produces almost every wine style found anywhere in the world. The port cities of Tarragona and Vilanova can supply rich and exquisite port and sherry styles plus any quantity of sacramental wines, while the western region of Lérida is home to truly California style Cabernets and Chardonnays. Priorato will outdo the Italian Super-Tuscan style in both quality and hefty price tags, while the highlands of Penedes will provide the outstanding wines associated with Burgundy and Germany.

If this isn't enough to satisfy the aficionado's cravings, the non-international style home-made wines from many small family bodegas throughout the region will furnish the true taste of Catalonia. Reds will be made from local varieties such as Tempranillo, Carineña, Ganarcha tinto, Monastrell and Sumat, the whites from Macabeo, Xarel-lo, Parellada, Ganarcha blanco or some specialty variety of the village.

In the main, these whites are meant to be simple everyday drinking wines at simple prices. By international standards they could be called austere, mainly due to low alcohol levels and being wine styles preferred by the locals who quibble about excessive oak, fruit or tannin. Freshness, read acid, is favoured even over fruity wines.

When enjoying wine at the source it is important to remember that wine is really about an accompaniment to food. And what the Europeans do best, and why there is a different style in each region, is that through centuries of experience they have developed wines that are considered ideal with their local cuisine. Enjoy

PROCESSING WINE

Except in countries with low labour costs — which will not last for long, the biggest percentage of grapes are machine harvested. These grapes go quickly to the winery in large gondolas. Otherwise hand harvested grapes are picked mainly into 15 kg plastic lug boxes which are easy to handle, stack and clean. Pickers are paid by the box and to avoid diseases, these boxes are disinfected after each use.

In the case of white wines, most grapes are pressed on the bunch in a horizontal tank press, the stems helping the juice reticulate in the press. Machine harvested grapes without stems often have rice hulls added to help the flow of juice between the skins. Then white juice, now known as *must,* is "settled" in a temperature-controlled, stainless steel tank allowing the solids to gravitate to the bottom of the tank, just as fresh orange juice deposits its solids in a glass. After 24 hours settling, the juice is then pumped to a fermentation tank leaving behind the unwanted solids, yeast's are added to start the fermentation process which converts wine sugars to alcohol making wine. The desire is to separate the juice from the skins as early as possible.

Black grapes are treated differently. As stems, seeds and skins all contain aggressive tannins like cold black tea, although the tannin of each is different, the desire is to avoid stem and seed tannins at all times. Berries are de-stemmed in a machine with spinning fingers and then drop to a carefully placed set of rollers which gently break the skin of the grape without crushing the seeds that would release unwanted bitter tannins.

The juice and broken berries are now the red version of must and is pumped to fermentation tanks with a choice of many different designs. Nowadays, the preferred choice is stainless steel, the same as white wine fermenters, however, some artistic types prefer the traditional epoxy lined, open top concrete tanks which have been used for eons.

The juice of most black grapes is much the same colour as lemon juice, the wine colour coming from extracts in the skin. Unlike white wine, it is important that the skins and juice are kept in contact but nature does not work like that. As the juice ferments it produces about equal parts of alcohol and carbon dioxide gas. This gas wants to literally lift the skins to the top of the must causing a "cap" of skins sitting on top. If left this way the wine will become nothing. Several methods are used to get the two components back in bed together, the most common being pump-over whereby the must from the bottom of the tank is pumped over the top of the skins several times daily.

A newish technique is a roto-fermenter, a horizontal rather than upright tank, which is mechanically rotated at regular intervals. The traditional method known as "pigage" is either foot-stomping the grapes or placing a plank across the top of the tank and manually punching down the skins with a plunger. There is now a machine version of this plunger. This process allows the must to obtain the necessary extractives such as colour, tannins and flavours from the skins.

The must is removed from the skins when the wine contains the desired amount of extractives. This is called free-run and the balance called pressings as the skins are then pressed to obtain the remainder of the juice. These pressings may or may not be added back to the wine. That is a very personal year-by-year, style-by-style decision. The dried skins are then returned to the vineyard as mulch.

*Above - grapes arriving at the winery are first weighed
and then tested for sugar.*

Below - stainless steel tanks - some idea of size.

Lug boxes are clean and efficient.

Red wine pressings.

The white grape Chardonnay is commonly fermented in 225 litre oak casks, a method which helps integrate the oak flavour with the fruit, making the wine more complex. This small scale handling as opposed to 5-10,000 litre stainless steel tanks adds considerable cost to the finished wine. With the fighting varietal wines, it is almost standard industry practice around the world to compensate for this smoky flavour by adding oak chips in large tea-bag like containers to the stainless steel tanks during fermentation. While this may be a similar flavour at a very favourable price, it is by no means the same thing.

Stainless steel tanks are inert, wooden barrels allow a small amount of oxygen to enter the wine which becomes the catalyst for numerous, favourable chemical changes that add subtle complexities to the wine.

White wine is usually bottled early to retain its fruity flavour and zest, then, in many cases, given some months of maturation in the winery. The first reason is to recover from what is called "bottle shock" after bottling and also to allow for some chemical changes in the wine - no wine before its time! The Catalan joven (young) wines are rushed to the market soon after bottling with the recommendation that they be consumed within the first year of its short life.

The more complex barrel-fermented wines normally don't get to the market before 18 months after harvest and are best consumed after three or even several more years in the bottle.

Much the same applies to red wines. At economy prices, few wines see the inside of a barrel for any reason. They are bottled early and despatched to retailers shelves with gusto. In fact, the largest number of red wines in supermarkets are but a solitary year old. So what, they taste good.

Higher priced bottlings go via a different route. These are normally meant to be cellared for a few years, anything from 3 - 30 years, the mainstream wines from 5 - 10 years — if there is any general rule. This maturation period allows the wine to chemically evolve and soften, the evolution providing greater complexity.

At birth, these wines are probably more tannic, maybe more alcoholic, and contain more extractives from the grape skin. These are further complexed by ageing in mainly new oak barrels which provide more wood tannins plus the barrels allow a small amount of oxygen to enter the wine. All these factors add-up to requiring time in the bottle or bottle maturation. This time of maturation is directly related to the amount of grape and oak extractives in the wine.

Oak casks are important in the scheme of things but it is folly to suggest that one type of oak is better than another. While white oak, whether it be from Russia, Austria, America, Hungary, France or wherever is the preferred type of wood for barrels, the author has seen excellent wines made in barrels coopered from chestnut.

Within certain guidelines, the source of the oak is far less important than the manner in which the barrel is made. Barrels can be bent to shape by steaming, boiling the timber or using a dry fire, each method extracts and provides different flavours to the barrel.

Then again, barrels are further "toasted" to retain (set) their shape and this toasting, depending on whether it is light, medium, heavy or charred (just like your breakfast toast!) really dictates the final flavours that the barrel will impart to the wine. The heavier the toast the more smoky flavours are evidenced, the less toasted give more pure oak/woody flavours. The amount of time a wine spends in barrel is dependent on the amount of fruit and extractives in the wine.

Again, this is all dependent on the percentage mix of new and aged barrels that have been used. Some wines go into 100% new barrels every year, this is largely reflected in higher retail prices. Most wines go into a three-thirds mix of casks, one third new, one third second year and one third old barrels. It is almost certain that the highest priced Catalan wines have been matured in 100% new barrels.

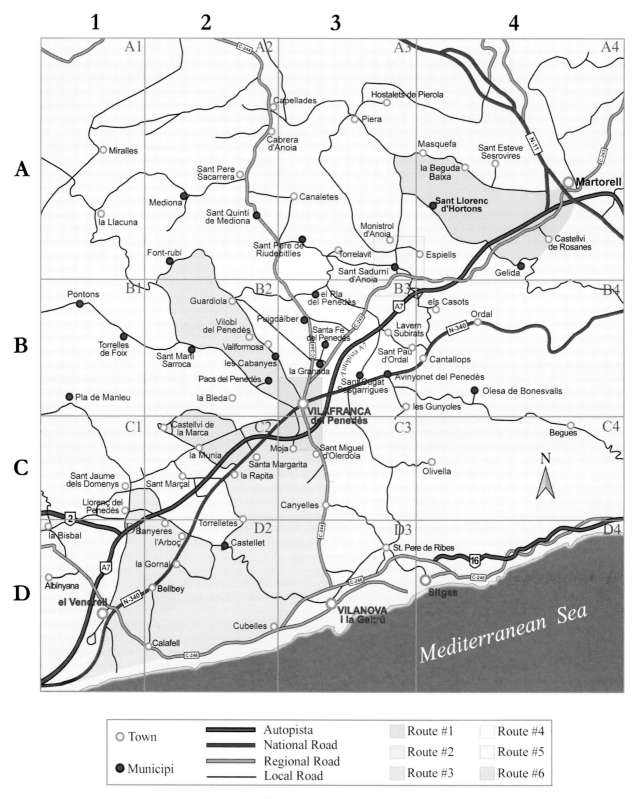

1   2   3   4

A1   C-244   A2   A3   A4

Hostalets de Pierola

Capellades

Piera

Miralles

Cabrera d'Anoia

Masquefa   Sant Esteve Sesrovires

A

Sant Pere Sacarrera

la Beguda Baixa

Martorell

Mediona

Canaletes

Sant Llorenç d'Hortons

la Llacuna

Sant Quintí de Mediona

Monistrol d'Anoia

Castellví de Rosanes

Font-rubí

Sant Pere de Riudebitlles

Torrelavit

Espiells

Gelida

Sant Sadurní d'Anoia

B1   B2   B3   B4

Pontons

Guardiola

el Pla del Penedès

els Casots

Ordal

B

Vilobí del Penedès

Puigdàlber

Lavern Subirats

N-340

Torrelles de Foix

Santa Fe del Penedès

Vallformosa

Sant Pau d'Ordal

Cantallops

Sant Martí Sarroca

les Cabanyes

la Granada

Sant Cugat Sesgarrigues

Avinyonet del Penedès

Pacs del Penedès

Pla de Manleu

la Bleda

les Gunyoles

Olesa de Bonesvalls

C1   C2   C3   C4

Castellví de la Marca

VILAFRANCA del Penedès

Begues

C

la Munia

Moja

Sant Miguel d'Olèrdola

Santa Margarita

Olivella

N

Sant Jaume dels Domenys

Sant Marçal

la Rapita

Llorenç del Penedès

Canyelles

la Bisbal

Torrelletes

D2   D3   D4

Banyeres

l'Arboç

Castellet

St. Pere de Ribes

16

Albínyana

la Gornal

C-246

D

Bellbey

Sitges

el Vendrell

N-340

VILANOVA i la Geltrú

Calafell

Cubelles

Mediterranean Sea

C-246

○ Town	▬▬ Autopista	▢ Route #1	▢ Route #4
	▬▬ National Road	▢ Route #2	▢ Route #5
● Municipi	▬▬ Regional Road	▢ Route #3	▢ Route #6
	▬ Local Road		

Index to Penedès towns and map of six touring routes

50

TOURING THE PENEDÈS WINERIES

An index to place names

ROADS LEADING TO PENEDÈS
AND THE WINERIES

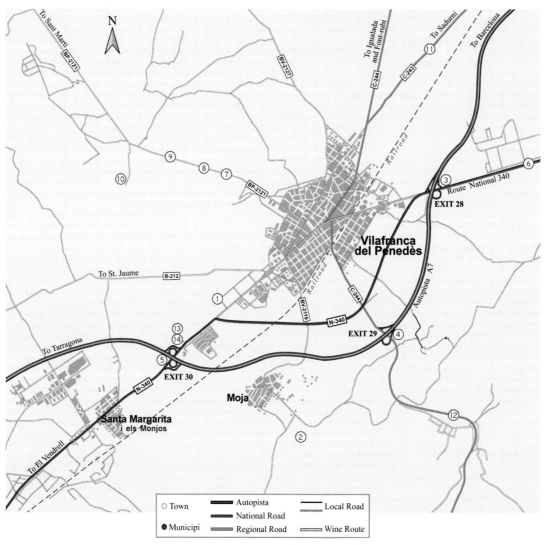

1. A. Mascaró
2. Cavas Hill
3. Exit 28 - north Vilafranca exit
4. Exit 29 - centre of village exit
5. Exit 30 - south Vilafranca exit
6. Route National 340 Barcelona - Tarragona.
7. Celler Cooperative
8. Mas Tinell
9. St. Martí, Pontons, Font-rubi road
10. Torres Visitor Centre
11. Sant Sadurni road
12. Vilanova i la Geltrú road
13. U.V.I.P.E.
14. Consejo Regulador

**NOTE - Only Exit 30 is open when travelling from the south. All three exits are available ONLY when coming from the north (Barcelona).

VILAFRANCA DEL PENEDÈS

Route #1

Includes: Greater Vilafranca del Penedès town, Moja and Pacs del Penedès

Scenic spots: Wine Museum (Museu del Vi) is a must! Allow at least three hours. Housed in the former palace of the Kings of Aragon-Catalonia, is arguably the world's best, especially for the history of wine in Europe and the Mediterranean . The tableaux and dioramas of winemaking since Egyptian times are outstanding as is the collection of Greek, Carthaginian and Roman amphorae. Tree-lined town square and Ramblas is the centre for most community activities, including many festivals throughout the year.

Wineries: Phone ahead for appointments

Morning:

Vilafranca City [C3]
Bodegas Pinord	93 890 0793
Bodegas J. Trias	93 890 2627
Antonio Mascaró Carbonell	93 890 1628

Moja-Olerdola 08734 [C2]
Cavas Hill	93 890 0588

Afternoon - a large choice:

Pacs del Penedes [B3]
Celler Cooperatiu	93 817 1035
at 1.3 km on St Martí Sarroca road BP2121	
Mas Tinell (next door to above)	93 817 0586
Miguel Torres at 2.4 km	93 817 7487
Cellers Grimau-Gol	93 818 1372

Vilafranca's world-class museum has many displays. Roman amphorae are prominent.

Restaurants:
While compiling this book, Hotel Domo was our base and we were happy with the food at the hotel's restaurant, authentic Catalan and international food, good local wine selection. A friendly hotel, all reception staff speak English; however, the accommodation is relatively expensive. For something very different, *Restaurant La Posada*, tel: 93 892 13 99, Sant Pere Molanta is a knockout - take a taxi. Another interesting spot close to town is Restaurant El Trull. For more formal dining, *Casa Joan*, opposite railway station.93 890 3171

CITY CENTRE & KEY POINTS

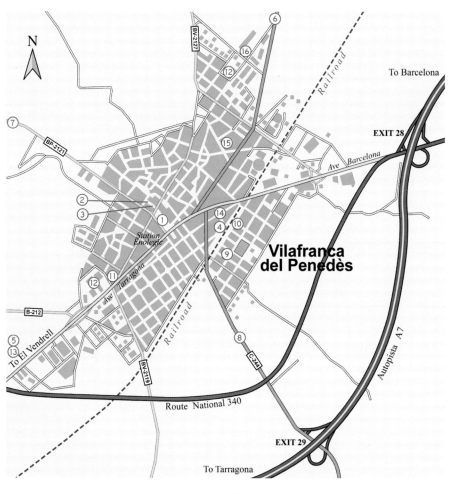

Legend		
○ Town	▬▬ Autopista	▬▬ Local Road
	▬▬ National Road	
● Municipi	▬▬ Regional Road	▭ Wine Route

1. City Centre
2. Tourism Office
3. Wine Museum
4. Rail Station
5. Consejo Regulador office
6. Sant Sadurni d'Anoia road
7. St. Marti Sarroca road
8. Vilanovi i la Geltrú road

9. Bodegas Pinord
10. Torres Administration
11. Hotel Domo
12. Markets (2)
13. U.V.I.P.E.
14. Bodegas A. Mascaró
15. Bodegas Grimau Gol
16. Hospital

CELLAR COOPERATIVE -PENEDÈS

Normally one associates co-operatives with the lowest wine common denominator, old concrete tanks, oxidized wines and inefficiency. This image has almost done a complete back-flip, and nowhere more successfully than just 1.3km from Vilafranca centre at the local co-op, or to use their equally long-winded Catalan name Celler Cooperatiu de Vilafanca del Penedès, SCCL!

Arguably the world's most modern wine processing plant, it is bordering on the size and efficiency of the most modern refinery. The winery is quite a landmark when viewed from the western edges of Vilafranca.

From the moment the grapes are greeted at the front gate, computers start processing information about grape quality and chemical analysis.

From there to a remote controlled weigh-bridge and onto the unloading bins when more computers take over the processing - this is hi-tech stuff - and the future for wine quality and profitability for the 400 members of this flourishing co-operative. Despite an already enormous plant, building operations were in full swing as grapes were being processed for the last vintage of the 20th century.

The fact that the co-op does not have one oak barrel in their 10 million litre winery clearly indicates that they are in the cava and white wine business. So be it. That has been the Penedès of the past where white grapes have been the main sustenance and kept the rural dream alive for the average grape grower, of which there are many. The co-op members reflect the true faces of Penedès grape growing.

Production revolves around cava which absorbs 60% of the 10 million litre production, of which six million litres are sold to other cava producers. The balance of production 20% white, 10% rosé and 10% reds (non-oaked) are made from Cabernet and Tempranillo. To this time, Chardonnay has not found its way among the three local varieties. All wines are joven, young, relatively low in alcohol (11%) fresh, unwooded and the Co-op says that this is what their UK supermarket customers desire.

Glorifying the local sport of castelling, the Co-op has a Castellers label, a wine that fits the supermarket formula perfectly. The national home market absorbs 90% of production.

The co-op welcomes visitors, Monday-Saturday, 0830-1330 - 1630-2030 by appointment.

 At the time of writing the firm still had an office, warehouse and shop conveniently located in Bisbe Morgades Street, Vilafranca, open during normal trading hours, where wine purchases can be made.

1999

CRIANZA

GRAN
CIVET

PENEDÈS
DENOMINACIÓN DE ORIGEN
alc. 12% vol.
750 ml.

CAVAS HILL
MOJA · BARCELONA · ESPAÑA
EMBOTELLADOR: CAVAS HILL, S.A. · R. EMB. 382-B

Author's Choice

Tempranillo

FERMENTADO EN BARRICA DE ROBLE
CHARDONNAY
CAVAS HILL
PENEDÈS
DENOMINACIÓN DE ORIGEN
750 ml.
R.S.I. 30-406/B PRODUCT OF SPAIN. R. EMB. 382-B
alc. 12'5% vol.
EMBOTELLADOR CAVAS HILL S.A. - MOJA - BARCELONA - ESPAÑA

Cavas Hill

As the name suggests, Cavas Hill, a company of just two shareholders, has English roots. Although very little survives of the origins of this elegant bodega - with its petite fountain and glorious views through almond trees onto sloping vineyards. A recently discovered document makes reference to the bodega's original English founder. Currently Cavas Hill produce 40% still wine and 60% cava, although this figure is tipping in favour of still wine, and in particular red wine that represents roughly twice the output of white.

The bodega counts on 50 hectares of its own vineyards. The rest of the fruit is bought, entirely in Penedès from another 100 ha that Cavas Hill supervise. Total production is about 1200,000 cases equally divided among wine and cava. Cavas Hill owes it success largely to a careful plan of attack on the Spanish domestic market, where it does 80% of its trade. Although exports represent 20% of their business, they are keen to find new markets. Cavas Hill has been exporting its wines since 1995 and is finding ready markets in Germany, Denmark, Sweden, Germany, Belgium, Japan, now U.K. and Ireland - and even China. The Tempranillo, with its rich, varietal purity and good colour and flavour extraction, is proving a great success. Oenologist and viticulturist, Fran Wernet, has been leading the bodega into an increasingly cosmopolitan arena, and the fresh, clean fruit that the wines exhibit will no doubt rapidly attract overseas buyers.

There are many styles of wines available from this bodega, and you can see a constant striving for perfection, be it in the type of wine for the price segment they wish to attack, or packaging. Some of the varieties at the core of the current work are: Tempranillo, Cabernet Sauvignon, Merlot and Garnacha, which they grow themselves. They also buy-in some Syrah grapes.

The Blanc Bruc (named for a Montserrat peak) is a blend of Xarel-lo, Sauvignon and Chardonnay of which 20% spends some months in oak casks to produce an interesting wine. The Chardonnay is another good value-for-money style and 30% of this also spends four months in oak.

Above all, this winery shines in the way they use that wonderful Catalan grape Tempranillo. This grape stars in the varietal Tempranillo, the Rosada Castell Roc, fresh and fruity, which includes 40% Garnacha, and also in the Gran Civet which is 50% Tempranillo, 35% Cabernet Sauvignon and 15% Merlot. These are thoroughly good wines, all equal to medal quality in any exhibition.

In keeping with the bodega's conscious effort to upgrade its wines - and its image - as they seek deeper penetration into all markets, there is an attractive flourish of Mediterranean colours on the Cavas Hill labels.

Above - An elegant lady controls large and sophisticated machinery.

Below - The stone mask of Mascaró.

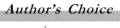

58

ANTONI MASCARÓ

Right in the heart of Vilafranca del Penedès you will find Bodegas Mascaró, behind a modern-looking portico emblazoned with a large stone mask, hence Mascaró (stone mask). The bodega you see today was founded by Narciso Mascaró in the mid 1940s. The Mascaró family has, however, been trading in bulk wine since half way through the 1800s. In those days they sold wine principally to Germany and Switzerland, always from Vilafranca. A booklet from 1919 shows that of 24 wine exporting houses based in Vilafranca, two belonged to the Mascaró family.

Antonio Mascaró, (mas-CAR-oh) the great-grand father, died of tetanus contracted from a barrel. His widow headed what was to become Viuda e hijos de Antonio Mascaró. She then joined forces with Josep Mascaró, her late husband's eldest brother. Josep had helped Cointreau, the French spirits company, to establish itself in Catalonia.

Josep's experience helped the family survive the Civil War by distilling alcohol as well as by the sale of bulk wine. Plans for a broader-based family business were put on ice during the war.

Finally brandy, a cava and an orange liqueur were produced as a first step towards a brighter commercial future. Slowly the brand name of Mascaró gained prestige.

Today the Calle Casal centre still acts as a family home and a cellar for red wine, as well as offices. In the Vilafranca industrial area you will find the grape crushing and vinification winery. When this land was bought the area was cheap since it was swampy ground and at that time useless for anything but ducks. Today it is slowly being absorbed by the urban sprawl of the expanding city.

Still wine production was begun by Antonio Mascaró in the 1970s. Now retired, it is his daughter, Montse, short for Montserrat, who runs the firm. A dedicated oenologist, she devours technical journals in Spanish, French, Italian and English and attends at least one technical conference abroad each year. In addition to being a mother, Montse is really attuned to what's happening in the fields of still, sparkling wine and brandy.

Initially, still wines were produced in conjunction with another company under the banner of Compañia Vinicola del Penedès. In 1990, Mascaró began to make wine, using only their own grapes. They have two vineyards with 40 hectares of vines. One is at El Castell seven km from Vilafranca while the other is called Mas Miquel. Once part of the Cistercian monastery of Santes Creus, it was forcibly sold by an act known as la Desamortización de Mendizabal, that affected Church property in the 17-18th centuries. When the Mascaró family bought the land the deeds were still in Latin.

The grapes grown here are used to make Sauvignon (blanc), Merlot rosé, tinto reserva Cabernet Sauvignon and a gran reserva called Ánima, Cabernet Sauvignon with 10-15% Merlot.

Since Montse began work at the bodega she has spearheaded a campaign to increase the company profile and to further concentrate on wines with that little bit extra. Her efforts have been crowned with success as customers now recognise that it is worth paying extra for anything with the brand name Mascaró. Tinto: Ánima, which can vary from 85 - 100% Cabernet Sauvignon, 24 months in American oak and three years in bottle, is quite a stunner.

Above - the bodega/warehouse facility near the railway station is functional, and on Carrer Dr. Pasteur. All Vilafranca street names are on attractive tiles.

Bodegas Pinord

The Tetas family, owners of Bodegas Pinord, have a long history in the wine business. More than 150 years ago they were already making and selling red and white wine, vinifying grapes from their estate in Sant Cugat Sesgarrigues. In 1942 José Maria Tetas inaugurated the present bodega, immediately adjacent to the railway station in Vilafranca, and just four km from the original finca.

With their central location in Vilafranca, Pinord give the impression of being a major presence in the region, an impression borne out by the facts. They have a capacity of five million bottles per year, using modern technology. Their product line is quite extensive, from cava, to still wines, to liqueurs, to dessert wines - all of this within a warm and happy family atmosphere. Some of this can be seen in how the company name developed; Pinord has an interesting history. On the northernmost boundary of the family's original vineyard there used to grow an immense and imposing pine tree. The family grew very fond of this great tree, and have used it as a symbol ever since. As it used to mark the northernmost boundary it was the northern pine, hence pin-nord.

Today Pinord has vineyards in different locations. Urban and suburban growth have crowded the original locations, forcing a move to other locations. Their main landholding is concentrated on two sites. Finca Muntanyans (35 ha) surrounds a small hermitage, called Santa Maria de Muntanyans. Fanning around it you can see Pinord's Xarel-lo, Macabeo, Parellada, Chardonnay, Tempranillo, Garnacha, Cabernet Sauvignon and Merlot plantations. Nearer Vilafranca, Pinord also own vineyards at Finca Coll de Bou (2.5 ha). Merlot was planted in this vineyard in 1991 and the vines are now bearing high quality fruit.

Pinord's rise to fame and fortune began when they started to make their petillant vinos de aguja. So successful were these wines some forty years ago that a slow but unceasing expansion program followed. The Cava revolution benefited the bodega greatly, allowing the introduction of stainless steel and cold fermentation technology. The benefit was first seen in the rising quality of red wines. As demand for red wines grew, so too did Pinord's expertise at producing them.

Clos 15 is a 100% Merlot that has spent three months in new oak. This light oak treatment combines fresh, supple Merlot fruit with a kiss of wood. The idea is to present a deep, red wine that can be enjoyed young. Although it is at its best after about 12 months, the wine does have some ageing potential. After two years the wood is still fresh on the nose, the fruit still vibrant. Still, it is best to enjoy this wine early.

Chateldon is the name given to reservas and gran reservas. The blend in this wine is principally Cabernet Sauvignon with up to 15% Merlot. The reserva spends one year in oak, sometimes a touch more, and then two years in bottle. Up until recently gran reservas were simply reserva wine that had been allowed greater ageing. Now, gran reservas are being made as such from the outset, from carefully selected barrels. These wines spend two years in oak, prior to another three in bottle.

José Maria Tetas and his wife recently celebrated their Golden Wedding anniversary, surrounded by over fifty Pinord employees. Their next project is a new bodega in Priorato.

61

Above - Pinord's back door, proves that nobody has a monopoly on traffic problems. If you have lived with them through a Civil War, these daily inconveniences are inconsequential. The front door (below) shows a dash of the family's class - and reflections!

Mas Borrás
Pinot Noir

12,5% vol
e 75 cl
Producido y embotellado por Miguel Torres, S.A.
Vilafranca del Penedès - Barcelona - España
PENEDÈS
Denominación de Origen

The true courage and entreprenureal spirit of the Torres bodega (and Miguel A. Torres) is shown in the story behind these labels.

The fact that top Pinot noir can be successfully produced in Spain is evidenced by this quite startling wine from the Mas Borras vineyard.

To show that Spanish varieties are not neglected at the Torres establishment, this Tempranillo wine at right is but one of 15 wines made solely or blended from other varieties. In some cases, 15% of "foreigners" are added - as with Coronas.

13% vol   PENEDÈS
Denominación de Origen   e 75 cl

Author's Choice

Grans Muralles

The Chardonnay from the Milmanda vineyard in the adjoining DO of Conca de Barbera so stunned the wine world that it brought about a totally new concept in Spanish, and indeed, European wine laws. Even though made in Penedès, this wine was ineligible for a label of that DO, and has instead a DO Conca de Barbera label.

Mas La Plana, 100% Cabernet Sauvignon, from a vineyard of the same name near the winery, is one the world's truly great wines of this variety.

Above. Very low-tech visit of wine afficionados from around the world visit Torres experimental vineyard at Mas Rabell which contains Spain's most extensive collection of local grape varieties. Below. Very hi-tech control of every winery operation is controlled by computer systems like this.

MIGUEL TORRES

So many complimentary stories have been written about the firm Miguel Torres SA - and Miguel A. Torres the man - that it is difficult to believe that anything new can be written about either. Yet, if there ever was a moving target, this is it; something new is always happening at this Spanish wine industry leader.

Torres would, unquestionably, rank as one of the world's three great innovative wineries along with California's Robert Mondavi and Penfold's of Australia All three are big and have a widely diversified product range with excellence at every level. There is no need to discuss specific wines from these companies as every one is a winner although Torres, arguably, offers the best value for money.

Each one of the five Torres generations has contributed something very positive, with a strong emphasis in the field of wine marketing; have wine, will travel. However, it was the much revered Miguel Torres Carbo of the last generation who gambled most by allowing today's Miguel A. Torres to revolutionize Spanish wine standards. He introduced French grapes, viticulture and winemaking methods into a traditional dyed-in-the-wool Catalan house. Much has been written about this fascinating story so we will bring the saga up-to-the first minutes of the 21st century.

Miguel A. Torres is a perfectionist with a clairvoyant sense, a man forever expanding every wine boundary. Wine and food matching is always under the microscope at the firm's own fine private restaurant; he is author of six tomes on viticulture and winemaking, and it is fair to say that he brought Chile out of the winemaking darkness by establishing his own winery there and setting completely new standards for Chilean producers. In addition to guiding the tra-

tional restrictive DO structure into competitive thinking (as president of the U.V.I.P.E. and prime promoter of this book), this human dynamo has worked out a joint winery venture, in of all places, China. Currently, Penedès bulk wines (same as Sangre de Toro) are being sent there and bottled in China under the Tres Torres label. Vineyards will be planted when sales indicate that these wines are fully accepted in the market. Yet this only a scratch on the surface of what's happening in the life of Miguel A.

The most exciting event will be reflected in many wine glasses the world over. The establishment of a new vineyard in the hazelnut mountain slopes of Priorato (on the back cover) will bring a totally new dimension to world wine standards. While Torres has been the champion of Spanish grape varieties - they have, arguably, the world's foremost Spanish vine collection, their international prestige has been attained through world-beating Cabernet Sauvignon, Chardonnay and Pinot noir wines. The Torres Cabernet Sauvignon and Chardonnay have humbled the best of France in events judged by Frenchmen in Paris!

Priorato will bring many changes. Garnacha tinto and Syrah are being planted on a mountain slope that's ideal for goat grazing. It is good to know that the future of such a dynamic company is assured. Daughter Mireya, a Montpellier oenology graduate like her father, is employed in quality control and a son is waiting in the wings.

Brother Juan María is also involved in an important executive position and all are working towards the company's mission of staying leaders in the Spanish industry, remaining a family company and increased product consistency. A winelover should never be disappointed with any of Torres more than 30 products.

Chardonnay

COMERCIAL ROVIROSA
MAS TINELL

Immaculate is the first word that comes into one's head as you drive into this father and daughter, rather young, establishment. Built in 1989, Mas Tinell is surrounded by vineyards and well-tended gardens, in vivid contrast to the awesome Vilafranca co-operative next door.

The first decade of Mas Tinell - meaning a little old barrel - has been one of incredible advancement even though they specialize in only two white wines and two cava wines. On the drawing board as we write is red wine production. It will be a pleasure to see what this capable, and dynamic pair will produce when they branch out into what seems to be the future for Penedès wine.

It is often said that too many cooks spoil the broth. This is not the case at Mas Tinell where both father and daughter are trained oenologists. Eva Rafecas, pictured on page 44, earned a degree in biology at Barcelona University and then a Master's Degree in oenology at the same university, a talented lady and this shows in the wine quality. Her father, Pere Rafecas, studied oenology at Requena. To watch them work together at harvest time is akin to watching the crew of a top rowing crew; it is all so rhythmical and looks just too easy.

The wines rely on cava base wine production style and methods and this is vindicated by considerable success in national and international competitions.

Mas Tinell Blanc de Blancs is a blend of Macabeo, 30% Xarel-lo, Parellada and 10% Chardonnay. These are fermented in temperature controlled, stainless steel tanks at an optimum temperature of 18 degrees celsius for 25 days to retain all the wonderful flavours of these four grapes. The colour is normally pale gold with an attractive tinge of green and in the mouth flavours of green apple and sometimes banana can be found. These young wines are best consumed within the first year after release. Normally they are about 11% by volume of alcohol.

The 100% Chardonnay is made in a similar way - same style tanks, same temperature but the fermentation goes on for 30 days. The aficionado will note flavours of pear, green apple and a little melon in this wine which normally carries about 12% by volume of alcohol, a rather standard level in these parts. It would be of interest to see the results of further fruit ripening by another 1% and see how this changes the style.

Under the Vino Tinell and Cava Mas Tinell labels, Mas Tinell currently exports to Denmark and Argentina from their limited production of 25,000 cases of cava and 3,500 cases of white wine. These wines will not disappoint even the severest critic.

Visitors are welcome by appointment Monday - Friday 0900-1200 and 1500 - 1800. Also limited weekend visits.

Maritime Penedès

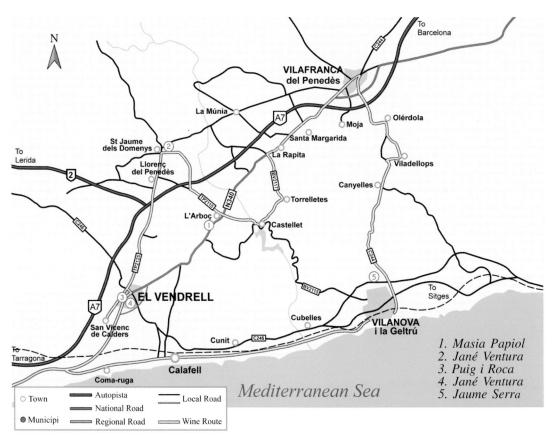

1. Masia Papiol
2. Jané Ventura
3. Puig i Roca
4. Jané Ventura
5. Jaume Serra

The town of L'Arboç del Penedès overlooks N340 and the crosroads from Castellet

MARITIME PENEDÈS

Route #2

A year-round scenic wonderland; less than 90km round trip.

Includes: Castellet i Gornal, L'Arboç del Penedès, St Jaume dels Domenys, Llorenç del Penedès, El Vendrell, Coma-ruga, Vilanova i la Geltrú, Canyelles.

Scenic spots: Outstanding castle at Castellet. Fabulous view of Penedès Valley from Sant Vicenç de Calders. The Roman Arch at Bara, 2,000 years old and still going strong.

Directions:

Take N340 (south) through Santa Margarida and just after La Rapita take BV 2117 (east) follow to Torrelletes continue to Castellet. Take TP 2115 west crossing N230 at L'Arboç del Penedès to St Jaume dels Domenys, Llorenç del Penedès > then TP 2125 to El Vendrell. Ask at local CIT for maps and directions. From El Vendrell take N230 for 4 km to Bara where you will see the Roman Arch of Bara, next to a nursery which has good parking. Take C246 through the many beach resorts to Vilanova > C244 > over the Garraf Range to Canyelles and Vilafranca del Penedès.

Wineries: Phone ahead for appointments

Castellet i la Gornal 43720	*D2*	
Masia Puigmoltó	Tel: 93 89 1076	
L'Arboç del Penedès 43720	*D2*	
Cooperativa Agricola L'Arboç	Tel: 97 767 0353	
Masia Papiol	Tel: 97 767 0056	
Sant Pere de Ribes		
Vega de Ribas	Tel: 93 896 0024	
Sant Jaume dels Domenys 43713 C1		
Coop. A. i C.A.	Tel: 97 767 7135	
Llorenç del Penedès 43712	*C1*	
Cai CA Llorenç del Penedès	Tel: 97 767 70226	
El Vendrell 43700	*D1*	
*Jané Ventura -	Tel: 97 766 0118	
right in town centre - ask for directions to:		
*Celler Puig i Roca	Tel: 97 766 6910	
Sant Vicenç de Calders scenic high point - has an historic wine press still used annually.		
Coma-ruga Archway & beach		
Vilanova i la Geltrú 08800	*D3*	
*Jaume Serra	Tel: 93 265 1551	
Vins Valldosera	Tel: 93 743 1175	
Viladellops-Olérdola 08734	*C3*	
Viladellops Vinicola		
Olérdola 08734	*C3*	
J. M. Torres Blanco	Tel: 93 890 1870	

Restaurants: Restaurant Pi - El Vendrell, classic European style, right on Rambla in middle of town ; Restaurant Victor - Coma-ruga, fully glazed, sidewalk café with fabulous views of beach and sea.

A winter view of the Puig & Roca vineyards at El Vendrell which are watched over by the historic village of Sant Vincenç de Calders.

PUIG I ROCA

José Puig is quite a celebrity within the large and increasing circle of people and wine lovers who admire him. When Miguel Torres first arrived in Chile, ready to unwittingly kick-start what is now regarded more or less as the Chilean miracle, it was to José Puig that he turned to in order to manage his winery there and to supervise wine-making.

Years later, the ever inventive and engaging José turned his hand to another aspect of the wine world that had always been close to his heart: how to get a cork out of a bottle. The resulting Puig-Pull is an invention that will delight any collector of corkscrews.

Keenly aware of the Roman heritage so clearly visible in Catalonia, and the fact that the great Via Augusta used to run right past his vineyard, the partners use Imperial Roman names to describe their vineyards, and wines.

In the vineyards his partner, Emil Roca, grows Cabernet Sauvignon, Chardonnay, Merlot and Cabernet Franc. The production is not large, 11,000 cases. The vineyard was planted in 1984, first crop was taken in 1989.

José's approach to oak is worthy of attention. He believes a wine should be allowed to reach just that point where oak begins to make a real difference, and no further. He uses both new and used barrels, and cares for them lovingly.

He makes around 2,500 cases of surprisingly good Chardonnay, "People used to say I was mad, planting Chardonnay so close to the sea." The brilliant quality of his wines attest that José is not mad.

When you step into the cellars of Puig i Roca you come up against an immaculately kept space full of 300 litre hogshead barrels. Each barrel has a little towel carefully placed at its head, containing the descriptors José uses to identify each barrel. "Toffee, orange, caramel, smoke," is written on one. Another reads, "Christina, you're an angel," (because this barrel went like an angel from the very first day).

"When one goes well you can almost forget about it, when you come back to it you go, wow!" says José. "Its incredible, every year is different. I do constant *batonage* (stirring the wine). If the barrels had any bad taste I couldn't do this."

José makes some of the only 100% Cabernet Franc in Spain, and it is a wine well worth seeking out. The Augustus red is made with 85% Cabernet Sauvignon and 15% Merlot. The smell is warm and typically varietal, with the fruit edging towards peppers with a cassis base. The flavour reveals a wine with good concentration.

Recent Augustus wines are similar in blend, but have even greater concentration and powerfully explosive fruit in the mouth. The critical success that their wines have attracted means that Puig i Roca could sell all their wine overseas. The partners insist, however, that 55% should be sold in Spain, because they believe that one's success must always be well anchored at home.

Never one to take life lying down, José has two other sidelines that are worthy of mention. He makes and sells some of the best gourmet vinegar imaginable, which he also uses to makes vinegar-flavoured chocolate bonbons to die for. Expansion includes a developing vineyard in Priorato about which everybody is very excited.

A pleasant place to spend a day at work! The restored 17th century El Padruell castle and a 21st century swimming pool.

Author's Choice

Granate Merlot

JAUME SERRA

Jaume Serra's owner José García-Carrión is a Jumilla, Murcia, tycoon with beverage interests all over Spain, among them the country's second largest selling wine brand Don Simon. Sr. Carrión has an extraordinary sense of selecting people and places. The Penedès winery of Jaume Serra is a classical example of this man's genius. Now one of the top 10 producers in the region, the brand name was originally founded in 1943 by oenologist Jaume Serra Güell in Alella, a small DO just north of Barcelona.

Enter the sherry producing family of Ramón Rato, who in 1956 purchased the 17th century El Padruell castle at Vilanova i Geltrú. In 1975 the Rato family bought-out Jaume Serra in Alella and in 1984 moved everything lock, stock and barrel to Vilanova. What has happened since is almost too good to be true.

Adjacent to the A16 autopista, this facility is attractively enormous by any standards and an acknowledgment of modern technology. Commanding a wonderful view of Vilanova and the Mediterranean, the bodega is as modern as tomorrow within the grounds of an old castle. The renovated castle is in pristine condition, complete with blue swimming pool. The whole scene reminds one of a fantasy holiday resort and the workers think it is a terrific place to spend a day!

For many reasons, most wineries have neighbours close-by. This winery with its 125ha of vineyards is isolated and could be considered an orphan in the Garraf Range due to the terroir problems of so little land being arable. None of this has stopped Jaume Serra from producing first class wines and cavas. The location is an arid, rocky, tough piece of real estate but the company has spent wisely on research as to what vines that will do well in this location. With this knowledge, Serra made 15 year contracts with independent growers to supply the needed varietals from selected regions.

The company finances 50% of the cost of planting the right varieties and controls the growing process, then buys the entire production at market prices. Many major wineries adopt a similar system of grape purchasing. Serra's own vineyards are planted to Cabernet Sauvignon, Tempranillo, Merlot and Chardonnay.

The winery contains almost 2,500 oak casks used in producing their admirable range of red wine products under the labels Jaume Serra, Viña del Mar and Cristalino. This bodega is oriented 75% towards wine and 25% to cava. Following an excellent 1998 harvest the company introduced a new red label range called Granate which will be reproduced every time there is a top quality harvest. These wines, all joven, include a Tempranillo which is a gutsy wine with good tannins and fruit that, although a joven wine, would be best with about three years bottle age when taken home. Other wines in the Granate range include Cabernet Sauvignon and Merlot while the Jaume Serra range has a Reserva, Crianza, Merlot, Cabernet Rosada, Tempranillo, Opera Prima Blanco seco, Xarel-lo and Macabeo.

Red wines represent 35% or 170,000 cases, of production, white wines 25% and rosé 15%. The main export market is the USA.

Visits are available by appointment.

BLANCO SECO

Opera Prima

PENEDES
DENOMINACION DE ORIGEN
PRODUCE OF SPAIN
Elaborado y embotellado por Jaume Serra S.A.
Finca El Padruell. Vilanova i la Geltru. Catalunya.
España

e 75 cl. 11% Vol.

OOPPERARAVINTOLAT/AMICA

R.E. 2020/B

JAUME SERRA

Author's Choice

Granate Merlot

XAREL.LO
Penedès
DENOMINACION DE ORIGEN
Blanco Semi-dulce

PRODUCE OF SPAIN
EMBOTELLADO POR: JAUME SERRA
VILANOVA I LA GELTRU. ESPANA

75 cl e
10.5% VOL.

JAUME SERRA

Below - photo-journalist Harold Heckle trades comments with winery director Javier Brunet.

Viña del Mar
AZUL

TINTO
COSECHA 1997

PENEDÈS
DENOMINACIÓN DE ORIGEN

Embotellado por:
Jaume Serra
Finca El Padruell.
Vilanova i la Geltrú.
Barcelona, España.
PRODUCT OF SPAIN
R.S.I. 30.4395/CAT
RE 2020/B

12 % VOL.
75 CL.e

JAUME SERRA

Merlot 1998

Penedès
Denominación de Origen

Product of Spain
Embotellado por Jaume Serra
Vilanova i la Geltrú.
Cataluña. España.
R.E. 2020/B

75 cl e 12% vol.

Masia Papiol

Located right in the town of L'Arboç del Penedès on the scenic Route #2, Mas Papiol fits snugly into this quite ancient setting. L'Arboç is well- known for its metallurgical industries, cereal, fruit and olive production as well as a large wine co-operative.

The local church dates back to 991AD and in 1147 Count Ramon Berenguer 1V gave the town to his sons; how nice! In between this gift and the foundation of the church, sometime in the 11th century, the Papiol family were first involved in the land. Signed bill of sale documents of February, 1076, retained by the family show that Castell de Castellet was transferred to the Counts of Barcelona. Other 16th century documents show the family lineage, heirs and heiresses through centuries of marriage and family viticultural land holdings. So it appears as though today's Papiol family have some legitimate claim to making wine and cava for sale.

The wine and cava are bottled under the Sant Ponç label and the range includes two white wines in 750 ml bottles while the two cavas can be obtained in three sizes up to three litre Jeroboams.

The big three Penedès white grapes, Macabeo, Parellada and Xarel-lo are the foundation of all wines although some Chardonnay is used in the cavas and the Grand Vino Blanc. The regular Blanc de Blancs still wine is in the normal hock shaped bottle and for some strange reason, probably easy identification, the Grand Vino Blanco which is one percent higher in alcohol, is in a Bordeaux bottle.

Visits by appointment.

Author's Choice

Cabernet Sauvignon

JANÉ VENTURA

Set in a very attractive location at an altitude of 200 metres above sea level, the vineyard Mas Vilella of Jané Ventura in La Bisbal del Penedès, eight km from El Vendrell is like a small chateau. At its heart is a lovely restored 17th century masia. The history of this bodega goes back to 1914 when the grandfather of the current owner began dealing with wines in bulk. This incredible building has age-old underground tanks containing 25 million litres of very cold water which is circulated and used for temperature control in the winery.

There is still a bodega right by the railway in El Vendrell, established in 1933, expanded in 1970 and again in 1988. It was where the father and grandfather of the current family used to load wines directly onto the railway. The building still contains much of the technology used way back then, before the current road system existed.

In those days it was a bonus to be either close to a port or next to a railway to be able to move wines to market. Current owners, Benjamí Jané Ventura and his sons Albert and Gerard, began bottling D.O. Penedès wine in 1985.

Albert sees new market trends leading towards the production of new wine styles. Although the majority of the bodega's business today is in the white and rosé markets, ever more red wine is being produced, and some new style whites are being bottled. The first red, a 1988 Cabernet Sauvignon wine, appeared in 1992.

Around finca Mas Vílella they have planted 11 ha of grapes, mainly Cabernet Sauvignon. Higher up, at an altitude of 400 metres on Els Camps estate situated in La Juncosa del Montmell, Ventura's own a 50 year old vineyard. This comprisies eight ha of Tempranillo producing wines of intense flavour and structure - and also Macabeo grapes. White and rosé wines are principally destined to the domestic market, while the reds are being largely exported.

At the moment the family produces roughly 1,500 cases of red wine to 8,000 cases of white. To complement the range, there is a project to make Macabeo and Xarel-lo wines with around 13% alcohol, greater skin contact and increased structure. Five hundred cases of this interesting wine style have been made and was released for sale at the turn of the century. Currently the bodega's wines are sold in Germany, Switzerland, Denmark, Sweden, Japan and the USA.

The Ventura's new-style white, the Macabeo was tasted just as it went into bottle. It is exciting and a different approach, and a true ambassador of fifty year old vines that can only give a small yield. A higher alcohol level of around 13%, with 40% of the wine being in oak for five months - the balance of the wine was sur-lies in stainless steel tanks during that period, indicates that this is a revoluntionary approach to making white wines in Catalonia.

One interesting aspect of the vinification of this Macabeo is the preference for larger 300 litre hogsheads of American oak. "I am not the only one, though," says Albert, "they are sufficiently sought after now that we find it difficult to get barrels delivered when we want them." Clearly the Ventura's are forming part of a renewed trend back to US oak, with significant results.

PENEDÈS VALLEY & HIGH PENEDÈS

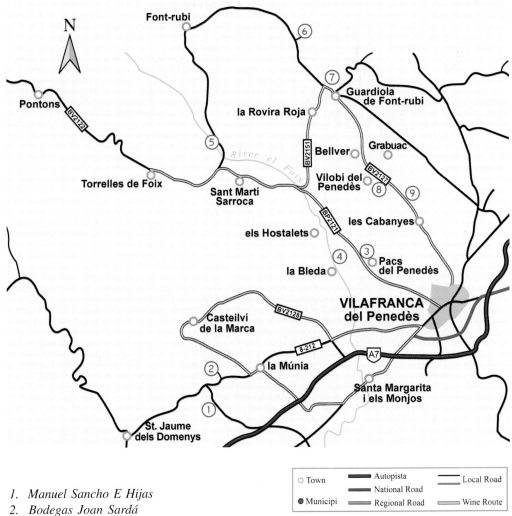

1. *Manuel Sancho E Hijas*
2. *Bodegas Joan Sardá*
3. *Cavas Parés Baltà*
4. *Rovellats*
5. *Mas Florit*
6. *J. Masachs*
7. *Cavas Ferret*
8. *Mas Can Mayol*
9. *Masia Vallformosa*

PENEDÈS VALLEY & HIGH PENEDÈS
Route #3

Includes: Santa Margarita, la Munia, Castellvi de la Marca, les Cases Noves de la Riera (morning), Pacs del Penedès, Sant Martí Sarroca, Torrelles de Foix, Font-Rubí, Guardiola Font-Rubí, Vilobí del Penedès, Les Cabanyes, returning to Vilafranca del Penedès

Directions:
Enjoy a late breakfast and take this morning drive to one more castle and lots of undulating country. Take N340 (South) to Santa Margarita les Monjos, at roundabout take BV2176 to La Munia - turn left (no sign) for 200 metres then right to Castellvi for a town visit. You will see the castle on top of a 470 metre hill. Then continue to BV 2176 and return to Vilafranca for lunch; the trip is only 30 km. Follow this with an afternoon in the high country, more scintillating scenery and as you climb the gorges you will see the remnants of now deserted vine terraces - you can guess the age and fate of these old vineyards. Afternoon trip a mere 50 kilometres through some fascinating country. Take BP 2121 to Parés Baltà at 4.8km; continue on through Sant Marti Sarroca, Guardiola Font-Rubi, Vilobi del Penedès, les Cabanyes and return to Vilafranca

Scenic spots: Castellvi de la Marca, Sant Martí Sarroca and Font-rubí

Restaurants: Sant Marti Sarroca is probably Penedès' top eating spot: - St. Jordi-Ca la Katy 93 899 1326 and Cal' Anna 93 899 1408; are two formidable restaurants by any standards.

Wineries Morning:
Santa Margarita i els Monjos 08730   C2

Joan Baques Lopez	93 898 0852
Jose Ferret Mateu	93 898 0105

Castellvi de la Marca 08732   C2

Bodegas Berdie Romagosa	93 891 8133
Grimau de Pujades	93 891 8031
*Manuel Sancho E Hijas	93 891 8281
Mas Lluet	93 891 8153
Pere Rius	93 817 0534
*Bodegas Joan Sardá	93 891 8053

Wineries Afternoon:
Pacs del Penedès 08796   B2

*Cavas Parés Beltà	93 890 1399
Josep Colet Orga	93 892 0637

La Bleda

Domingo J. Marti	93 898 0113
*Rovellats S.A.	93 898 0131

Sant Martí Sarroca   B2

Antonio R. Torné	
Remei Fabré Queraltó	93 899 1071

Torreles de Foix 08739   B1

*Mas Florit (on Font Rubi rd)	93 899 0121
Exploitations V/v del Penedès	93 899 1359
*Josep Masachs	93 899 0017

Font-rubí   A2

Cellar Can Surio del Castell	93 897 8426
Heredad Mont-Rubí	93 897 8552
Juliá Navinés	93 897 8358
Pere Olivella Galimany	93 897 8202
Joan LLopart Pons	93 898 8156

Guardiola de Font-rubí 08736 B2

Jaume Llopart Alemany	93 897 9148
*Cavas Ferret	93 897 9148

Vilobi del Penedès   B2

*Masia Vallformosa	93 897 8286
*Masia Can Mayol	93 897 8001

Les Cabanyes 08794   B2

Bodegas Masia Sague	93 892 0850

The winery, complete with TV antennae, is guarded by the 10th century Castell of Pujades.

Left - the white chalk soils of Castellvi show-up the summer-pruned leaves and bunches.

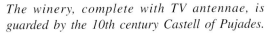

Author's Choice

Cabernet Sauvignon

1995

Joan Sardà

CABERNET
SAUVIGNON

PENEDÈS
DENOMINACIÓN DE ORIGEN

Embotellado por Bodegas Joan Sardà,SA
Castellvi de la Marca
Made in Spain

75 cl.   12,5% vol.

BODEGAS JOAN SARDÁ

Bodegas Joan Sardá was founded in 1927, by *abuelo* (grandfather) Tomás. Abuelo Tomás began with a vineyard and a small bodega that produced more wine than he could distribute locally. As Barcelona was reasonably near, he used a horse and cart and set about distributing to his friends and acquaintances in the big city. The bodega then passed onto Joan Sardá, who in turn passed it on to his son Joan, the father of the current owners, Antonio and Juan.

They possess 10 hectares, planted with Cabernet Sauvignon and Chardonnay, with some recent plantings of Merlot. Most of the wine made at the bodega is still wine. The proportions are roughly 70% red wine to 30% white. The vineyards now reflect a planting policy of 60% Cabernet Sauvignon to 40% Merlot. Antonio and Juan Sardá both work together as oenologists. As a youth, Antonio worked on the farm part-time as he completed his studies in oenology.

The fruits of this hard work are reflected in wine styles that fit in well with today's market requirements. The proof of this is seen in exports to Canada, USA, Japan, Cuba, Costa Rica, Germany, Denmark and even Perú, Denmark, Russia and the Ukraine! The domestic market takes 70% of their wines, of which about 80% are distributed within the region of Catalonia; the rest is sold in Madrid and the north.

When evaluating the wines of this bodega you soon come to the conclusion that these folks really love their red wines. The whites tend to trail somewhat sadly behind. A good example is a white called Blanc Mariner. The wine is made of 60% Parellada and up to 40% Chardonnay. The bought-in Parellada may have let the side down a bit, as it is not as crisp and lively as it might be. Their early Chardonnay Joan Sardá is not favourable on the nose, either. Although it has a great acidic structure it never quite manages to leave you totally convinced.

Try the reds, however, and a whole new vista appears. The Cabernet Sauvignon rosé is bright, light cherry to look at, lively and aromatic on the nose, with all the charm and depth of a good varietal nose that translates fully in the mouth. A good wine!

When it comes to the Tempranillo, the Sardá brothers seem to like maturity, for in their crianza, the nose comes out with all the aromas of maturing fruit. It is a clean wine, which means that although the barrels used are second use, they have been looked after and kept clean. In the mouth the wine is soft, much as a mature Tempranillo should be, and its finish leaves you with a round feeling, touched by an impression of clean, sweet fruit typical of good glycerols.

Their Cabernet Sauvignon red wine exhibits all the benefits of owning your own vines. Aromatically this wine delivers all the beauty inherent in Cabernet Sauvignon. It is bright, black-currant-laden, with hints of capsicum and peppermint. In the mouth it has a lively, almost New World (dare one say Chilean?) quality to it.

As you might expect, the brothers also have a more mature wine to show. Their Gran Vinya Sardá Reserva is made from 100% Tempranillo aged for one year in 300 litre American oak barrels. The wine is clearly made from low yield vines because the colour, despite its years, is still dark red with a lovely cherry edge. To the nose the wine presents lovely ripe fruit cucooned in clean oaky smells. It is a thick, enveloping wine, very aromatic, clean and lingering, and very good.

Above - all roads lead to Cavas Ferret. The statue is a memorial to those who died in the Civil War. Below - father Ezequiel Ferret O. and son Rodrigo, in charge of marketing.

Xarel-lo

Xarel.lo

Ferret®

PENEDÈS
Denominación de Origen

Embotellador Ferret S.A. Guardiola de Font-Rubí
Alt Penedès • España
12,5% vol   R.E. 2206-B   75cl

CAVAS FERRET

Cavas Ferret, established in 1941, are situated in an imposing bodega that includes the family residence with extensive gardens. The masia-cum-bodega looks straight down the main street of the pretty little village of Guardiola de Font Rubi, just nine kilometres from Vilafranca.

The name Ferret is not uncommon in Penedès wine lore and it isn't easy to resolve which bodega is which, particularly as a sign outside this house indicates there is another such named bodega 3 km away in Font-rubi. Unfortunately, as happens in so many family wineries around the world, a family disagreement saw the eldest son leave the fold and start-up on his own after 22 years of being involved in the family business.

It has been my pleasure to meet with them all several times, and as they are all very nice people, it is satisfying to report that both parties are doing well in their own rights. With time, one hopes they will learn that blood is thicker than cava and this feuding will resolve itself - for the benefit of all.

Cavas Ferret owns 10 ha of mainly Parellada grapes in the uplands of Font-rubi hence their desire to purchase more land. Although the production is 70% cava (nearly 17,000 cases) they have attractively packaged varietals of Xarel-lo and a Cabernet rosada. Unlike the Blanc Sec which is the standard cava base wine at about 11% alcohol, the Xarel-lo is made as a still wine with 12.5% alcohol meaning that the fruit was fully ripe and this shows in the wine. The Xarel-lo has good mouthfeel and lots of potential. As the family comes to understand the international market and makes more of this Catalan wine style, they are on a winner.

Red wine blend for the Reserva (only 200 cases) is 50% Tempranillo, 28% Cabernet and 22% Merlot while the crianza is a Tempranillo 50%, Cabernet 26%, and Merlot 24% blend for which they have 200 oak barrels. These are definitely wines to be watched.

In addition the wine production is divided equally (10% each) between white, rose and red wine which totals 5,000 cases. The highest quality is this family's only criteria.

While father Ezequiel takes an active part in the organization as CEO, the day-to-day operations are in the hands of two sons, a very bright young Rodrigo in charge of marketing and elder brother Ezequiel who looks after production. They are generous and pleasant hosts serving excellent wines.

Cavas Ferret's principal markets are in Catalonia and Spain with exports to Germany, UK, Japan and small quantities to the USA. Future plans call for the purchase of more vineyards so that they can control the supply and quality of their grape intake while slowly growing in export markets.

Visitors by appointment Monday- Friday 0900-1300 & 1500-1800; w/ends 1000-1400.

Above - Joseph Masachs is a top-class presentation, from vineyards and wine, to lawns and labels.

Below - viticulturist Joan Masachs and oenologist Pere Pons.

JOSEP MASACHS

Travel on the Sant Marti Sarroca road, and immediately after the turn-off to Guardiola Fontrubi take the next right turn for three kms along a concrete road lined with olive trees to this quite spectacular bodega of Josep Masachs.

There is an air of calm efficiency about this modern-looking bodega which, in fact, was established in 1940. The gates open electronically as you arrive and inside everything is spotlessly clean and running like clockwork. Neatly tended lawns and gardens surround the buildings and the adjacent 32 ha of vineyards are just as carefully tended.

This is the style of the Masachs' winery, most especially because it is the way the two brothers in charge like to do things. They are tall and soft-spoken, with young and cosmopolitan families. This is the third generation of Masachs to make wine, and they are determined to be up to with the leaders in every way.

In terms of still wine, the brothers have adopted the same forward-looking approach. Precision moulds are used to shape their bottles, and sunken corks give their wines a modern look. "There is always a desire to move things forward, and we are never slow to re-style," says Regina Elias, responsible for international sales. In keeping with this image, the sales force - seven for Spain and two for overseas is young.

Blanco Seco Josep Masachs is made with Xarello, Parellada, and some Muscat of Alexandria to lift the flavour a touch. The bodega also produces mono-varietal Chardonnay that encapsulates typical, citrus and peach character. The wine is well made and definitely benefits from some

extra time in bottle. After a year in bottle the Chardonnay character is more forward, softer, more buttery, though still retaining a firm acidity. This is a superb wine, among the best produced in Spain.

Josep Masachs make an unoaked, single varietal Cabernet Sauvignon. Aromatically, this wine is varietally well focused. In the mouth it is full and austere, a wine for a formal dinner. Bottle age also becomes this wine, it opens very pleasingly after a year and a half in cellar.

"With Spain in a favourable economic position, one can see this is a good moment for our products," say the brothers. There can be no doubting their words.

This same modern, cosmopolitan air is evident inside the winery, where stainless steel and high technology refrigeration systems produce wines that eventually sell in Holland, Germany, Denmark, Sweden, Finland, England and Scotland. With more than four million bottles in permanent stock, this is no pint-sized operation. Masachs' will shortly be selling in the USA.

Annual sales are running at around 200,000 cases, placing Josep Masachs in equal fourth place in Catalonia in terms of production; not bad out of a total of some 278 producers. Having said that, Masachs still concentrate on their core business, which is supplying the domestic market, where 85% of their wine is sold, albeit cava is their leading product. The wine sector is split is 18% white wine, 15% red and 4% rosé and 63% cava.

Week day visits by appointment - 0800 - 1200 and 1500 - 1700

MAS FLORIT

Mas Florit is owned by the Parunella family of Barcelona and farmed in conjunction with Jordi Valles who is also the on-site manager, viticulturist and winemaker. Jordi Parunella senior, his three sons and their families who all work in their own professions in Barcelona. They all visit the 17th century masia every weekend. Eldest son, predictably Jordi (whose son is also Jordi), works in with a giant international corporation. Another son Carles is a surgeon and there is a third son Jaume.

The business arrangement between the Parunella and Valles families, where the grower is part of the business, is one of the last of what was a traditional relationship in Penedès.

Even though it is exactly 12 kilometres from Vilafranca on the Font-rubi road, Mas Florit is not easy to find on the first visit. If you reach the old church you know you have gone 100 metres too far, just backtrack to the first dirt track and take the one on your right. A tiny sign will lead you to the masia.

The oldest part of the masia dates back to the 14th century and stretches underground for three metres. This is the place where the wine was traditionally made.

Grapes produced from the 47 ha vineyards far exceed the needs for Mas Florit's own wine, about 4,000 cases, so excess grapes grown on the property are sold to all-comers. There are plenty of takers as the masia has developed a fine reputation for top quality fruit.

The white wines comprise a Blanc de Blancs and a Xarel-lo varietal made very much in the cava base wine style. These are good wines, nothing outstanding, yet the Xarel-lo with a touch more alcohol, would be the choice. However, it is the Tempranillo crianza that stands out among the still wines. This is no whimp, rather a big, hearty red. Lots of mouth-filling Tempranillo "muscle" and tannin, a wine that will still be in good shape for your yet unborn daughter's wedding!

Visits by appointment.

MAS CAN MAYOL

Mas Can Mayol is another bodega that is not so easy to find. The reason is that it nestles within its own extensive vineyards, and is some way off any bitumen road. At the moment it is very much a winery with work in progress.

A new vinification plant is being constructed by the Mitjans family and building is proceeding slowly but surely with señor Mitjans senior in charge of works. The great advantage here is that the impressive vineyards have been in the family for five generations.

This means that a profusion of good quality fruit is available. Currently there are 40 hectares of Cabernet Sauvignon, Merlot, Chardonnay, Xarello and Pinot noir. Sauvignon (blanc) and Chardonnay are bought-in from vineyards higher up, at Pla del Manlleu. What is notable is the significant amount of Pinot noir planted, a rare sight in this vicinity.

Another intriguing fact is that the underground cellars, now used for ageing wine, began life as air raid shelters for the Republican Air Force during the Civil War. At that time, some of the family vineyards were commandeered and made into an airfield where Russian-made fighters would take off to protect Barcelona from attack by Franco and the Luftwaffe. Joan Mitjans, the family oenologist, can still locate the dynamite holes that would have destroyed the place in the event of it being over-run by Nationalist forces. Today this space protects 450,000 bottles in cool and quiet safety.

Two brands have slowly been making a name for themselves in markets as far afield as Belgium, Holland, the UK, Mexico and the USA.

These are Masia Can Mayol and Loxarel. Small quantities have even been exported to Benin - wherever that is!

Loxarel Tempranillo sin (without) crianza (being in oak) is macerated for 18 days at 24°C, having been de-stalked prior to light crushing. The wine has good structure, an earthy feel about it; an artisan product with its feet on the ground.

Different vintages of this wine give a very good account of the quality of the harvest. A good year is far more generous with its rich fruit. Another style is made up of 80% Cabernet Sauvignon, 20% Merlot. This wine is aromatic and also a sin crianza. Lovely glycerine levels give this wine the impression of brimming over with sweet fruit, albeit it is really quite dry.

Loxarel Cabernet Sauvignon is 100% Cabernet and spends 12 months in 300 litre barrels. This gives it a great aroma, mixed wood and fruit elements. This is a wine to lay down for a while, as it is certain to improve, but is perfectly approachable while young.

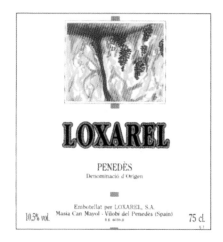

PARÉS BALTÀ

NORTH WEST MEDITERRANEAN WINE

1997 CABERNET SAUVIGNON RESERVA

750 ml.e   PENEDÈS   12,5%vol.
DENOMINACIÓN DE ORIGEN

EMBOTELLADOR: CAVAS PARÉS BALTÀ S.A. - PACS DEL PENEDÈS - PRODUCT OF SPAIN

R.E. 2043- B1   R.S.I. 30- 3326

PARÉS BALTÀ

1790   1934

NORTH WEST MEDITERRANEAN WINE

Mas Elena

1997

PENEDÈS
Denominación de Origen

 75 cl.   ELABORADOR PARÉS BALTÀ, S.A. -PACS DEL PENEDÈS- ESPAÑA
R.E. 2043-B1

12,5% vol.

Author's Choice

Cabernet Reserva

NORTH WEST MEDITERRANEAN WINE

Honey Moon

1997   *Blanco*
Medium

1934   1790

PARÉS BALTÀ

PENEDÈS
Denominación de Origen

75 cl.   ELABORADO POR CAVAS PARÉS BALTÀ, S.A. PACS DEL PENEDÈS-ESPAÑA
PRODUCT OF SPAIN

10,5%vol.

R Emb. 2043-B1

CAVAS PARÉS BALTÀ

Currently, there are three generations of the Cuisiné (coo-zee-nay) family involved at Parés Baltà. Grandfather Joan Cusiné who's on the job at 6am daily ensuring that all the vineyard equipment is ready for when the workers arrive, father Joan Cusiné Carol, chief of operations, and his son, Joan Cusiné Hill, who is in charge of marketing.

Back in 1928 when aged 11, grandfather Joan started work in a Penedes vineyard for the princely sum of four pesatas per week. As a corporation, they now own three vineyards and a winery, offices in Madrid and Penedès.

At the start of the third millennium the family show all the trappings of success with sales to such diverse countries as Germany , Belgium, Holland, Denmark, Japan and Ireland. Other success indicators are a line-up of new Mercedes Benz and Range Rover vehicles!

Following the Civil War in 1940, grandfather Joan became a successful dealer of horses and cattle, a business that gave the family financial stability. A photo store was added in 1953 and the first vineyard purchased in 1958. By 1970 the family started making wine and selling it in bulk, still a common Penedès habit.

Realizing that success in the wine business was in the finished bottle product, the family purchased the Pacs del Penedès firm of Parés Baltà in 1978. Further vineyards were purchased in the higher regions of Pontons and Torrelies de Foix.

Present day chief Joan started his working life at age 16 teaching Spanish (and learning English) in Leicester UK for one year before returning to the family fold. Besides becoming a

winelover, like so many of his contemporaries, Joan became a "foodie" - a lover of the finest foods. He has accompanied his mentor and friend, famous San Sebastián gastronome and writer Rafael García Santos, on gourmet trips to many countries.

Joan believes that this wine/food affinity has sharpened his wine skills and has now adopted the motto of "fruit in the glass" as the company's motto. He teaches wine subjects at the Cambrils Institute of Culinary Arts and restaurant technology.

He is a firm believer that Merlot is the heart and soul of Penedès red wines while Cabernet Sauvignon and Cabernet Franc both are seen as essential to top quality reds.

Joan thinks that old-world wineries have not generally kept pace with winelovers demands. This belief took him to Australia and his son to the USA in search of new ideas and practices. Parés Baltà also imported Australian viticultural whizz, Richard Smart, to help with vineyard technology and practices, and another Aussie, Michael Goundry to help in the winery.

While most of the red wine grapes are grown around the Pacs del Penedès bodega, both Mas Carol (named for his wife) and the Pontons vineyards are the source of Chardonnay, Riesling and Parellada white wine grapes. Amiable oenologist, Magdalena Gallart, crafts these grapes into some of the best wines in Penedès.

The *Honey Moon,* a slightly sweet wine, is a successful attempt to reach out to Generation X while the more conventional wines, both oaked and unoaked are quite incredible value-for-money wines with appeal right across the board.

Above - the main cellars and chapel.

Left - Maria Rosa Cardona.

BLANC
DE
BLANCS

ROVELLATS
PENEDÈS
DENOMINACIÓ D'ORIGEN
ELABORAT I EMBOTELLAT PER ROVELLATS S.A.
LA BLEDA - SANT MARTÍ SARROCA - ESPAÑA

ROVELLATS

Rovellats is a bodega set within a very special environment. At the heart of the bodega lies an imposing 15th century Masia. You will see history in its every detail, from the gardens to the chapel and further-on into the caves. Its early beginnings as a family home, with a large, open hearth fire and a nearby wine press, are admirably preserved.

The masia is surrounded by one of the most attractive and genuinely romantic gardens in Catalonia and has lent its name to the local district. The brainchild of José Vallés Rovira, a past owner of the bodega, it exhibits numerous statues and plant arrangements all in a turn of the century Renaissance-inspired Romantic style, typical of post-Modernism Catalonia.

Not surprisingly, the garden and chapel are a very popular location for wedding receptions and anniversary celebrations. The gardens are well kept and mature, giving the bodega a stately appearance and a unique and peaceful ambience. It is a place of great beauty in which to enjoy a glass of wine.

Prior to the late 19th century outbreak of phylloxera, the bodega produced still wines. Recovery from phylloxera involved planting Macabeo, Xarel·lo and Parellada and shifting production entirely to cava. In recent years a single still wine has been added to the range, Rovellats Blanc de Blancs. Naturally, it is a white wine combining the three traditional grapes of Penedès, plus a small percentage of Chardonnay to give the flavour a little added depth. This is a special, limited production wine. Each year 2,500 cases are released , and recent wines have shown maturity in their yellow-golden colour, leading to a nose with fruit and yeasty breadth to it. This is an approachable and pleasing wine with a long and satisfying finish.

Deep underground there is what might possibly be the only star-shaped cellar in Spain, and owners Rosa Vallés Casals and Juan Cardona Parés suspect it might even be unique in the world. It really is a sight to behold. Rosa is formidable lady of class and tireless in her job as a vivacious promoter and marketer, assisted by her lawyer trained daughter, Mª Rosa Cardona Vallés .

The only down side to this beautiful garden location became apparent on the 10th of October 1994, when a downpour of biblical proportions caused the small stream (which gave Rovellats its name) running beside the bodega to burst its banks and inundate the star-shaped underground cavas. The rainwater touched the very roof of the cellars. No bottle was left unscathed. Being October, the bodega was in full preparation for its Christmas sales campaign, loaded high with cases of wine ready for market. When the flood subsided the bodega was left with nothing. Winemaking son, Josep Cardona, had to rush to the local store to buy a new hammer and an adjustable spanner. It took three years to put the devastation right.

Rovellats has 140 hectares of Macabeo, Parellada, Xarel-lo and 1.5 hectares of Chardonnay. Harvest time is a particularly picturesque time at the bodega, with small, tractor-driven loads arriving amidst garden scenes that are truly memorable. Really, a place of joy, serenity and beauty.

Above - Rovellats popular chapel

Below - Rosa Vallés i Casals stands beside an unusual staircase made from cava bottles

PARATÓ

You can attack the Parató bodega from almost any direction as the roads from Sant Sadurni d'Anoia (8 km)and Vilafranca (10 km) both converge on El Pla del Penedès and the family estate of Can Respall de Renardes. This is the home of Parató wines which was established in 1975. Although at least 40 km inland from the Mediterranean, you'll be bewildered by the sight of a giant ship's anchor, in very good condition, set in among 94 ha of vineyards. Sorry, no explanation, except that the owner likes anchors - while the vineyards are at an average height of 350 metres above sea level!

Parató is unusual in another way in the it is probably the only winery that makes the red/white combination of a 100% barrel fermented Xarello - and 100% Pinot noir as their lead wines. Pinot is rather thin on the ground in these parts, however, my notes indicate that these are good wines. Montserrat Elias yet another talented Catalan lady, sister of manager Josep Elias, is a trained veterinary surgeon who also holds a Masters degree in oenology from Barcelona University.

Add to these a Negre Clàssic, made from 80% Tempranillo and 20% Pinot noir, and a Blanc Coupage made from 50% Macabeo, 30% Xarel-lo and 20% Parallada and the aficionado is well catered for with a different range of good wines. The red wines are fermented on skins for a minimum of 10 days at a controlled temperature of 27 degrees celsius and then spend at least 12 months in barrel.

The whites are bottled young to preserve fruit character and freshness while the reds are barrel aged in American oak to develop their own character and depth. The Parató Negre Classic is 30% Crianza and 70% Reserva.

A recent addition has been the Tinto Renardes, a blend comprising Cabernet and Tempranillo. The early wines were 11.5% by volume of alcohol. At this alcohol level the fruit was not fully ripe and this showed in the wine as high acid and low flavour. As their Cabernet vines age (planted 1990), Parató has wisely chosen to pick later when alcohol levels are around 12.5%. and this has increased flavour, balance and mouthfeel. Even higher levels of maturity will be beneficial to this style.

Total production from this energetic family runs around 8,500 cases. Visitors are welcome by phoning ahead for an appointment.

93

"Up on a lofty bluff, imperiously dominating the landscape it surveys, there is an old, castle-like structure with a very warm and homely air about it - Can Feixas".

The brothers Huguet.

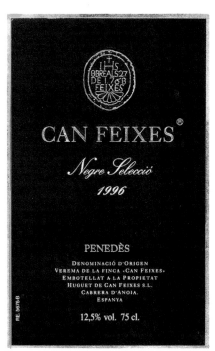

CAN FEIXAS - HUGUET

The government road builders have recently smiled kindly on this hospitable Huguet family by constructing a high speed road to Canaletes making it quite simple to visit a top quality producer who welcomes visitors. Make sure you take the new road one way and then take the old route through Sant Quintí de Mediona on the return journey. This is classic Penedès.

Up on a lofty bluff, imperiously dominating the landscape it surveys, there is an old, castle-like structure with a very warm and homely air about it that is actually a fascinating winemaking establishment, Can Feixes. This is a bodega with a long history. José Maria Huguet, the current owner, still has documents dating back to 1400 that make reference to the bodega. If you think about it, Columbus still hadn't been born, and half of Spain was under the government of Islam. That is a long time ago!

The house that is now visible is actually the second owned by the Feixes family. The first forms part of the foundations of the current one. Wherever you look there are ancient pieces to view, doorways dating from 1790, additions from 1878, in short, a wonderful history and architectural lesson at every corner. At the beginning of this century the family name changed to Huguet due to the lack of male descendants.

If you climb up to one of the turret-like viewpoints on the house you can still see the arrow slits used in centuries gone by to defend the estate against attack by marauding raiders. Today, these are used by the birds for nesting.

Currently the family hold 330 hectares of land higher up the hillside, not adjacent to the property. Not all of this land is suitable for vines, and so only 70 hectares are given over to vineyard. Here the Huguets grow a type of Parellada known locally as Montonet - the mountain grape. Up at this altitude the variety achieves its maximum expression, its best identity.

They also have some Macabeo, that gives fruity wines with an interesting structure. Also grown are Chardonnay, Tempranillo which is called by its traditional Catalan name of Ull de Llebre; Cabernet Sauvignon, Merlot and Pinot noir.

The estate makes a total of around 15,000 cases a year. Of this, 4,000 cases are destined to cava, 6,500 cases are white and the rest goes into tinto crianza and reserva. About 60% of the production is sold on the domestic market, 40% is exported - mainly to Germany.

The Can Feixes Blanco Selecció is made from 50% Parellada, 20% Chardonnay, 8% Pinot Noir, and Macabeo. It is star-bright to look at and has a nice, lively nose with some underlying aromas reminiscent of olives.

Can Feixes Chardonnay is in individually numbered bottles, barrel-fermented and a wine of considerable merit, carrying normally 13% alcohol and lots of smoky flavour. The tinto, Can Feixes Negre Selecció, is a blend of 50% Cabernet Sauvignon, 40% Tempranillo and 10 % Merlot. Aromatically it is a winning wine, with a soft and light feel in the mouth, ideal for lighter meals. Later vintages of this wine are darker, more powerful and full of promise.

The family welcomes visitors by appointment - and, for many reasons of interest, this would be one very worthwhile visit.

Vallformosa is a place of beauty - from both within - and without.

MASIA VALLFORMOSA

If you follow the road that winds away from Vilafranca and leads to Guardiola de Font-Rubí, you soon come to the imposing location of Masia Vallformosa, on the right hand side of the road. Don't be surprised to find a hive of activity here, for this bodega is literally doubling its size. The reason for this expansion is that the Domènech family, owners of Mas Vallformosa, have acquired another two prime vineyards to add to the seven they already own. Of 600 hectares, they have 400 dedicated to viticulture.

The family's wealth comes from supplying base wine for the cava industry. Success in this field has prompted them to turn their hand to making their own products, including still wines. Hence the purchase of more land and doubling the size of their operation. The family, under the astute guidance of the father, has harnessed the energetic enthusiasm of the younger generation to build and consolidate ceaselessly.

Their land holdings are a sight to behold. The new ones are perched and neatly terraced high up in the Upper Penedès, ideal for aromatic wines. A great deal of work has gone into shaping and planting these new vineyards so as to take best advantage of every factor: grape variety, soil type, land inclination and solar exposure.

For red varieties that need greater amounts of sun, they have some beautiful vineyards within visual contact of the sea.

Don't be fooled by the workmanlike appearance of the bodega. The Domènech family own some of the prettiest properties in Penedès - old masias with stunning views and landscaped gardens that make you want to stay forever. A trademark of the family is the use of old-style *tinajas* and palm trees to adorn their gardens.

Masia Vallformosa is not a small outfit. Their wines are sold in more than thirty countries, including Central and South America. Their domestic sales force keeps a barometer on quality by also selling champagne Lanson on a national scale. Stainless steel technology is visible in the bodega, as are some of the newest nitrogen bubble filters available. The family's commitment to improving the quality and the value for money aspect of their wines is discernible here.

Vallformosa still wines are all good value wines, and bound to improve greatly as the new vineyards become productive. Viña Blanca is a white wine made from Macabeo, Xarel-lo and Parellada. It is not a base wine for cava as it is harvested later to avoid this style. An unoaked Chardonnay with a generous, varietal nose that definitely improves with bottle age is a very good deal. Vall Fort is a crianza wine made from 75% Tempranillo and 35% Garnacha, spending up to a year in American oak barriques. This is a fast-maturing wine with a traditional nose. Vall Reserva is a blend of 85% Tempranillo and 15% Cabernet Sauvignon. This wine also tends to deliver mature aromas, has a big structure and a long finish.

Masia Vallformosa makes wines to enjoy today, and will surely make wines to look forward to in the future.

Left - Masia Vallformosa CEO José Domènech shares a glass of wine with DO Penedès director, Josep Ribas.

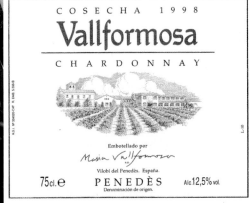

Below - the impressive horizon of Vallformosa surrounded by vines and magnificent gardens.

MANUEL SANCHO

Mont Marçal is one of the success stories of winemaking in Penedès. Beginning in 1975 with a small winery and a small production sold locally, it remained stable, as one of the many interests of a rich and successful owner, Manuel Sánchez. One could say it was run almost as a hobby. In 1985 it all began to change. Things moved pretty fast from there, with an accelerated interested that has yet to see a peak. The popularity of red wine has prompted the bodega to build a new facility at Cal Diabla, in Vilobí.

With 40 ha of its own vineyards, the bodega finds it has to buy grapes, and sometimes wine, to satisfy demand. Their vineyards supply Macabeo, Chardonnay, Parellada, Xarel-lo, Cabernet Sauvignon, Merlot, as well as Cariñena and Tempranillo.

Realising that traditional white wine in Penedès is just base wine for cava; a wine style popular in Catalonia because it is considered to be light, easy to drink and low in alcohol; they have decided to improve the product and bring it more in line with current international tastes.

The main reason for this strategy is that this type of wine is almost impossible to sell elsewhere. The oenologist, Pedro Muñoz is now intent on designing wines aimed at the European taste, wines with more alcohol and more structure. With reds, there are limits to what can be done because there isn't any Garnacha and Monastrell in their area. Developments are, hence, based around Cariñena, Cabernet Sauvignon and Merlot.

For the future they are looking at working to adapt the vineyards so as to produce grapes destined for wines with greater structure. Mont Marçal is also looking at different fermentation techniques. The aim is for longer fermentation times, added skin contact, more contact *sur lie*, i.e. leaving the wine in the barrel on its yeast lees. Mont Marçal Chardonnay is fermented in new American oak barriques.

Despite training as a white wine specialist, Pedro Muñoz has perfected quite an art at developing wonderfully aromatic red wines. The wine is full of fresh, rounded, deep flavours.

The crianza tinto is a blend of Tempranillo and Cariñena, with a touch of Cabernet Sauvignon. The Reserva is a more careful blend of 60% Cabernet Sauvignon, 30% Tempranillo and 10% Merlot. It has a soft garnet colour and an aroma led by more mature fruit. The flavour also gives the impression of ripe, mature fruit.

Penedès Valley

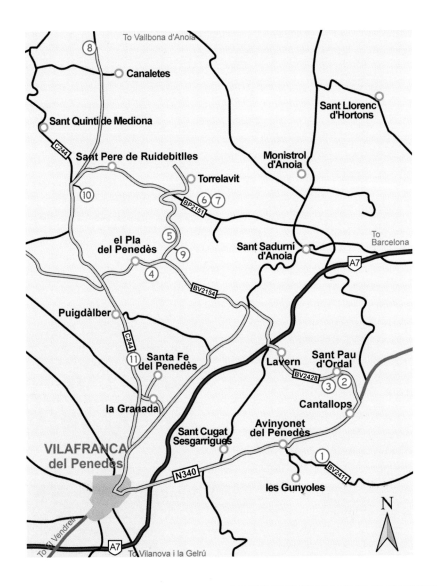

1. Can Ráfols dels Caus
2. Albet i Noya
3. Eudald Massoni Noya
4. Cellers Alsina
5. Jean Leon
6. Rene Barbier
7. Conde de Caralt
8. Can Feixas
9. Parató
10. J. J. Lluch
11. C.I.G.R.A.V.I.

○ Town	▬ Autopista	▬ Local Road
	▬ National Road	
● Municipi	▬ Regional Road	▬ Wine Route

PENEDÈS VALLEY
Route #4

Includes: Sant Cugat Sesgarrigues, Avinonyet del Penedès, Sant Pau d'Ordal, Lavern, Torrelavit (includes Lavit and Terrassola) Sant Pere de Riudebitlles, Sant Quinti de Mediona, el Pla del Penedès, Puigdalber, Santa Fe del Penedès, la Granada.

Scenic spots: An early start recommended! As you enter road BV2428 there is a good view across the Valley and also to Sant Pau d'Ordal and Lavern.

Directions: Take the N340 to Avinyonet where you will see sign to Olesa. Follow for 2.3km to Can Rafols. Return to Avinyonet, turn right on N340, follow through Cantellops to Sant Pau/ Lavern turnoff on left. Road BV22428 will quickly lead to Albet i Noya - a must stop. Leaving their gate turn left, through Sant Pau to E. Massana Noya, another good stop. From Lavern there are good views of the valley and Sant Sadurni on right - pass under the A7 autopista and railway. Come to C243, turn left for 150 metres, then right towards El Pla, first stop on left is Alsina & Sardá, Then take the windy road B2153 with superb views to Torrelavit. Turn right at BP2151 which follows a special little valley to Rene Barbier and Conde Caralt. Return along this valley road, through St Pere to new C15 road to Canaletes and Can Feixes. Return along this road to C244 which will bring you to J. J. Lluch and CIGRAVI wineries before returning to Vilafranca. Total distance 65 kilometres.

Wineries: Phone ahead for appointments.

Sant Cugat Sesgarrigues	*08798*	*B5*	**Torrelavit**	*08775*	*A3*
Chandon	93 897 0505		*René Barbier	93 891 7000	
Avinyonet del Penedès	*08793*	*B3*	*Conde de Caralt	93 891 7000	
Albert Milá Mallofre	93 897 0052		*Jean Leon	93 817 7400	
*Can Rafols dels Caus	93 897 0013		Sadeve	93 898 8691	
Les Gunyoles-Avinyonet	*08793*	*B3*	E. Nadal	93 898 8011	
Cuscó Esteve	93 897 0164		**Sant Quinti de Mediona**	*08777*	*A2*
San Pau d'Ordal	*08739*	*B3*	*Jordi Lluch Lluch	93 898 8138	
*Albet i Noya	93 899 4056		**Puigdalber**	*08789*	*B3*
*Eudald Massana Noya	93 899 4124		Antonio Garriga Mitjans	93 898 8166	
Bofill Rovira	93 899 3002		Gabriel Giró Baltá	93 898 8032	
Lavern-Subirats	*08739*	*B3*	**Santa Fe del Penedes**	*08792*	*B3*
Olivella Bori	93 899 3351		*Cia Int'n'l de GrandesVinos	93 897 4050	
Pedro Canals Casanovas	93 899 3202		Josep Jané Santacana	93 898 8205	
El Pla del Penedès	*08733*	*B3*	**La Granada**	*08792*	*B3*
Antoni Canals Nadal	93 898 8081		J.iP. Ponts Font, Elaboradors	93 897 4064	
Bodegas Capitá Vidal	93 898 8630		Masia el Mas	93 897 4251	
*Cellers Alsina	93 817 0177		**Canaletes**	*08796*	*A3*
*Parató Vinícola	93 898 8182		*Can Feixes Huguet	93 771 8227	

Restaurants: Village of San Pau d'Ordal: Cal Xim; on main road C243 to Sant Sadurni the Hotel Sol i Vi has a nice poolside restaurant.

Eudald Masana Noya

Eudald Massana Noya is situated on road BV 2428 in the prime locality of Sant Pau d'Ordal just west of the town. This friendly family set-up, established in 1917 and restructured in 1996, is destined for an excitng future. Records held at the monastery of Montserrat indicate that the Massana family have been involved with viticulture since 1777. Firstly, they make very good wine - without frills. The unwooded Chardonnay is among the region's best and sells at a reasonable price while the crianza Cabernet Sauvignon, which does spend some time in barrels, is also a worthy product which the family rates ahead of the Chardonnay. One cannot fail to notice that family wineries are dedicated to giving value-for-money.

Secondly, what appeals about the firm is the unpretentious manner in which they present their wines. Visitors by appointment are invited to enjoy the wines which are served from a barrel-cum-table outside on a delightful patio, complete with sun dial. This is a scene which many aficionados can see themselves as potential wine makers. For the budding amateur winelover who has the mad desire to become a professional, they could certainly equate with this charming scene.

With 30ha vines located in St. Pau and nearby Avinyonet del Penedès, production is slanted 70% towards cava. However, with a good range of local and imported grape varieties from Xarel-lo to Cabernet the family produces a worthwhile range of still wines including a rosé, red and white. A varietal Tempranillo is certainly worth seeking-out should the reader be visiting Spain.

Although Eudald Massana is the CEO, oenologist, and viticulturist, my visits revealed that he had some very charming and willing assistance from other members of the family.

At the time of writing, sales were restricted to Catalonia and Spain but future plans call for export action.

Weekday visits can be made 0900-1300 and again in the afternoon from 1400-1600. Saturday visits are available from 1400-1600 also 1600-1900. Visit on Sundays from 1000-1400, all visits by previous telephone appointment. In addition to the DO wines, an on-site shop also sells bulk wine and vinegar, eggs, onions, honey, olive oil, dried beans and wine glasses!

ALBET I NOYA

Owner and oenologist José María Albet i Noya is someone who has taken a long, serious look at wine, and studied it in depth. He has spent time learning from such luminaries as Australian guru, Dr. Richard Smart, and has come up with a style of making wine that will please even the most fastidious wine lover.

José María is extremely interested in the environment. As a result, he has opted for organic cultivation. He has even had a look at biodynamics, the most stringent of all farming methods. "For the moment that is too tough," he states. "But I think we should care for the environment as much as we can. That is why I still hand harvest grapes. We used a machine one harvest and found at the bottom of our tanks 1,800 kilos of locusts, grasshoppers, snails, slugs, various other insects and even three snakes!"

One wine that stands out and is slowly winning the acclaim it deserves is his Xarel-lo. To achieve this wine he has fermented some of the Xarel-lo in stainless steel with extended skin contact, and some in barriques, with batonage as it rests on its lees. "The wood I use is varied, but it includes about 80% American Tennessee oak barriques," he adds. The real secret is not here, though. "It is in the vineyard. If you smell the wine, then leave it in your mouth for about a minute," he says, "you will get aromas and flavours of orange peel, orange groves in blossom, and almond blossom." The grapes for this wine come from just one particular corner of a single vineyard he owns. "The earth suddenly turns very red. My brother can't yet do it, but my father and I can, we can actually smell these aromas in the vineyard. That is where this all comes from." It took José María ten years to perfect this wine, and it has been time well spent. It is a white wine that is glorious now, but improve even more in bottle, a rare gem. His Chardonnays are also wines to enjoy now or age for a couple of years.

Like van Gough, who took years to learn how to master drawing before venturing onto oil paints, José María has done the same with *assemblages*. "Everyone used to tell me that assemblages, or blends of varieties, were the ultimate expression of wine," he says. "But I wanted first to find out exactly what my wines could do independently, so as to know their character, really." His varietal Cabernet Sauvignons are earthy, full and deep, pungent with vitality and not at ready to release all their secrets immediately. Tempranillo is another grape that he has clearly come to understand. His blends are even better. These are a blend of five different grapes: Cabernet Sauvignon, Tempranillo, Merlot, Syrah and Petit Syrah, aged 12 months in barrels.

1997

GRAN CAUS

PENEDÈS
DENOMINACION DE ORIGEN

COSECHADO, ELABORADO Y EMBOTELLADO
EN LA PROPIEDAD
Can Ràfols dels Caus
AVINYONET DEL PENEDÈS
ESPAÑA

Alc. 13% by vol.   750 ml.

EMB. 5.476-B   L - 02 97 01   Can Ràfols dels Caus, s.l.

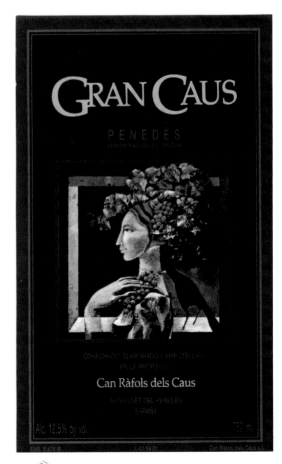

GRAN CAUS

PENEDÈS
DENOMINACION DE ORIGEN

COSECHADO, ELABORADO Y EMBOTELLADO
EN LA PROPIEDAD
Can Ràfols dels Caus
AVINYONET DEL PENEDÈS
ESPAÑA

Alc. 12.5% by vol.   750 ml.

EMB. 5.476-B   L-01 96 01   Can Ràfols dels Caus s.l.

CAN RAFOLS DELS CAUS

There is something ancient sounding about the name Can Rafols dels Caus. Perched on top of a hill, overlooking a truly splendid view of Penedès, this imposing masia adds to this impression by looking positively patrician. A few flourishes here and there, like a massive Calder-like steel mobile, an interesting weather vane and some noisy, exotic birds - gives the place a somewhat different feel, as if anything could happen here.

Originally part of a grand-paternal inheritance, the estate was divided among brothers 20 years ago, when for the first time it began to bottle its own wine. With 450 hectares, this bodega certainly has the land to make a significant impression in the wine market. However, for the moment it only has 45 hectares given over to vines, with a plan to possibly increase this to 60. Innovation and variation are themes that you easily recognise in this fascinating place.

No less than 22 different grape varieties grow in the vineyards. Tempranillo, Graciano, Monastell, Cabernet Sauvignon, Cabernet Franc, Merlot, Nebbiolo, Pinot noir and several mixed types of Garnacha grow to provide for the tintos. Xarel-lo, Macabeo, Chardonnay, Chenin (blanc), Sauvignon (blanc) and two types of Moscatel are among the white grapes available.

The wines made at this bodega give all the appearance of having been made with infinite care and attention to detail. Take, for example, the Gran Caus Blanc. The percentage of grape variety is carefully measured to provide exactly the aromatic and flavour combination sought by the winemaker: 45 % Xarel-lo, 40% Chardonnay and 15% Chenin (blanc), all at 13% alcohol. A nice, light yellow colour leads to a good mouthful of flavours and fruit. Some might say that this wine is over-complex, but the truth is that you can see that the winemaker has his eye on how the wine is going to age.

The wines made here are all made with a view to drinking now, but are ageing very gracefully into something even greater.

The Petit Caus, made from the younger vines on the estate, has 29% Merlot, 22.5% Tempranillo, 22.5% Cabernet Sauvignon, 13% Cabernet Franc and 13% Syrah. Deep purple in colour when young, it is still a remarkably bright and clean wine, and great value too.

The big brother Gran Caus vintages contain 36.5% Merlot, 30% Cabernet Franc, 17.5% Cabernet Sauvignon and 15% Tempranillo. It spends 11 months in barriques of Tronçais oak. Only 2,000 cases are made. These are deep, perfumed and gloriously maturing wines, if you can stop yourself from drinking them as soon as you buy them.

The labels that decorate the wines are a mixture of attractive and extravagant, all made by recognised artists. These wines age splendidly well, especially if you like wines that develop mature, leathery, deep-fruit aromas

Visiting hours - daily by appointment.

Merlot

CHARDONNAY

ALSINA & SARDÁ

PENEDÈS
DENOMINACIÓN DE ORIGEN

12% Vol. 75 cl.

EMBOTELLADO POR:
CELLERS ALSINA, S.L.
EL PLA DEL PENEDES · BARCELONA · ESPAÑA R.S.I. 30.4165 CAT · RE 5768 B

CELLERS ALSINA

Surrounded by beautiful, gently sloping vineyards, climbing roses and multicoloured flowers, Cellers Alsina makes quite an impact when one sees it in summertime. From its verandah you can see the vineyards sweeping away to distant hills, enclosing the macroclimate of the region. These 40 hectare vineyards contain Macabeo, Xarel-lo, Parellada, Cabernet Sauvignon and Merlot. At a higher altitude they also have some Chardonnay growing. Some grapes are also bought in.

This is a family company, born from the business union of two brothers, Alfonso and Juan Alsina Sardá. They sell most of their products on the Spanish market, but their exports are increasing in leaps and bounds. At the moment they export 20% of their production. These exports go principally to Europe, with some movement beginning in Asia. Red wines lead the export drive.

One interesting statistic is that the domestic Spanish market has a preference for Celler Alsina's rosé wines. Of a total production of 25,000 cases of still wine, rosé, or rosado as Spaniards call it, accounts for 30% of their production. Twenty percent is white, while red wine accounts for 50% of their output.

The Vino joven white is made from 40% Macabeo, 25% Xarel-lo, 25% Chardonnay and 10% Parellada. It is light, yet fruity. The Blanco Alsina & Sardá is a blend of 50% Chardonnay and Xarel-lo. It has quite a honeyed aroma, with a substratum of peach and pear. The 100% Chardonnay, unoaked, is again also honeyed,

pleasantly aromatic, with well focused fruit. An oaked Chardonnay has been added to their list.

The 100% Merlot has no oak, splendid fruit and excellent aromas, a wine much in keeping with modern consumer expectations. It has great concentration of berry fruit. Retailing at very affordable prices on the domestic market this wine represents excellent value for money.

A Cariñena and Tempranillo blend that sells for a very humble price on the domestic market also represents star quality at an economical price. It is a vibrantly bright wine with clear, fresh fruit showing right through it. There is an older tinto crianza style that relies on 75% Tempranillo and 25% Cabernet Sauvignon, with a touch of oak. This is a mature, dense, exceptionally well developed wine with hints of aniseed and damson fruit.

Another style on offer contains the reverse of the above, that is, 75% Cabernet Sauvignon and 25% Tempranillo. It spends one year in oak, and makes a fascinating comparison with the previous wine.

A wine designed specially for the On License trade, or restaurants, is the Tinto Penedès Alsina & Sardá. Ten percent Merlot rosé is blended into the Cariñena and Tempranillo wine described above. This gives the wine just a touch of friendly, cocoa-chocolate aromas and a soft mouth feel able to please most food-conscious consumers.

Phone ahead for appointments.

At the end of a long, dusty approach road there is a modest looking bodega with sloping vineyards on all sides.

Chardonnay

A rare photo of Jean Leon, the man who started it all.

JEAN LEON

1998
Chardonnay

PENEDÈS

Jean León

Nº 010050

JEAN LEON

Some wineries command legendary status. In the case of Jean Leon, this reputation is rightly gained. The story of Jean Leon goes back to the early 1960s, when an expatriate Spaniard, living in the U.S.A., became interested in making his own wines. Jean Leon had made his fortune as a restaurateur in the United States. He even provided the spread for Ronald Reagan's presidential bashes.

Jean harboured a dream to create his own wine to supply his restaurants. He knew he wanted the wine to be European - that was the style he chose - but he also needed the wine to exhibit all the modern thinking that was helping to revolutionise the American wine industry.

Initially Jean looked in France. Land was so expensive there, that he soon opted for alternatives. Some Catalan friends suggested he take a look at the viticultural potential of Penedès. He was sufficiently impressed to commission an in-depth survey of the region.

Jean was cautious enough to know that in winemaking and vineyard cultivation you need plenty of information. Soil and sub-soil studies and climatological analyses were compiled and sent to America for assessment. The verdicts were all exceptionally favourable and planting went ahead.

Jean Leon was a true pioneer in that he chose varieties he knew he could sell; yet they were totally experimental in Penedès. He opted for Chardonnay and Cabernet Sauvignon. Right from the start the rich, creamy, oaky Chardonnay proved an outright success. Rumour has it that sales staff were having to insist that buyers take three cases of Cabernet if they wanted one of Chardonnay.

The problem with the Cabernet was two-fold. First, there was the fact that the vines were young, and second was that these wines had been made to last. This rendered the young Cabernets so tight that they were rather hostile without bottle age. Maturity was to come, and with it came a pretty spectacular wine. Jean Leon's fame spread far and wide. It was not from all that far away, however, that the keenest eyes of all were watching.

At Miguel Torres, Jean Leon's progress was monitored closely. Torres had been considering planting these varieties, especially when a young Miguel Torres returned from studying in France to declare that he thought Cabernet Sauvignon was 'king', the variety to plant.

Changes at Jean Leon have taken place slowly but surely. The quality of the wines has risen as new investment in winemaking equipment and in the vineyards takes effect.

At the moment things look pretty much as they always have. At the end of a long, dusty approach road there is a modest looking bodega with sloping vineyards on all sides. Inside the bodega there is a certain atmosphere that tells you very good wines come from here. That impression is no mistake.

Visits by appointment.

Above - one of the hundreds of trailer loads of grapes that are inspected daily.

Please take a chair for our next performance!

RENÉ BARBIER
Mediterranean White™

WHITE WINE
PENEDÈS
DENOMINACIÓN DE ORIGEN

Alc. 11.5 % Vol.   75 cl e

PRODUCE OF SPAIN *Embotellador* RENÉ BARBIER, S.A. R.E. 243-B *Torrelavit* • *Spain*

RENÉ BARBIER
Mediterranean Red™

RED WINE
PENEDÈS
DENOMINACIÓN DE ORIGEN

Alc. 12.5% Vol.   75 cl e

PRODUCE OF SPAIN *Embotellador* RENÉ BARBIER, S.A. R.E. 243-B *Torrelavit* • *Spain*

RENE BARBIER

One thing you notice immediately as you approach the grand old stone masia of Segura Viudas (and also the home of René Barbier) at harvest time is the vast amount of grapes that come in for crushing. A very reassuring sight is that the grapes that do come in all seem to be ripe, and all well cared for. They arrive in 22kg boxes, loaded onto platforms behind tractors proudly sporting the Segura Viudas logo. The procession makes a big impact on passers by, as it give the impression that Segura Viudas is an important installation.

As you draw nearer, this impression is reinforced by the appearance of the bodega behind an imposing queue of immaculately kept tractors bearing their fruit to the press. Next to the stone masia there is a big white house, framed in large stones, with small white balconies and wrought iron work around the window frames.

There can be no doubt this is a solid and prosperous operation by anyone's standards. Manuel Durán, who is in charge of running the bodega, is a man of firm views, great dedication and a wry smile, masking a witty and dry sense of humour. The success of the wine-making businesses he manages is such that he can well afford to have a twinkle in his eye. His brands are known throughout the world.

The story of René Barbier has not always been such a happy one. After phylloxera made a mass of his business, exporting wines to Sweden from Valencia, he decided to re-locate to Penedès. Following a reasonably successful re-establishment, the company was purchased by Manuel Segura Viudas, founder of the bodega we see today. Later on, the firm was bought by Ruiz

Mateo's Rumasa group, an entity that absorbed huge amounts of Spain's wine making industry in the 1970s. The trouble with this set-up was that it literally grew too large.

Eventually it drew in important chunks of the financial sector, including banks, pension funds and massive real-estate complexes. The crunch came when the group fell foul, first of fiscal and fiduciary regulations, and then of the government.

As the Rumasa Group collapsed, taking with it, many people's hard work, savings, hopes and aspirations, the government was forced to step in to try and rescue what it could, and what it felt was financially possible. This included the Segura Viudas empire. Happier times returned when Freixenet, who Manuel Durán has helped steer to great prosperity, bought the government out.

Today René Barbier, and Conde de Caralt, a brand name used by the company, presents good value for money wines in numerous markets around the world. Constant experimenting leads to new styles of wine. There is a very intriguing Xarel-lo, fermented in 300 litre American oak barrels with medium-plus toasted French oak barrel heads.

Macabeo is another single varietal wine that is achieving interesting results, as are barrique fermented Chardonnays. New and very deep Tempranillos are well worth trying to find, and the Tempranillo and Garnacha blend is a real winner.

For a more mature experience, the Gran Reserva René Barbier is certainly value for money.

Th world's largest tractor parade performs for two months every year at Conde de Coralt.

Author's Choice

Vendimia Seleccionada

CONDE DE CARALT

Conde de Caralt is yet another label of the giant Freixenet cava and wine group.

The most remarkable success story in Penedès centres around the marriage of Dolores Sala Vivé to Don Pedro Ferrer. Both had deep and abiding interests in wine. He was particularly good at selling, while she was an enormously talented technician. She could recognise wines, blind, by terroir, a feat still difficult today. In 1925 they decided to pool their talents and began making cava. As of that moment, the future of the Ferrer family was set.

Having said that, the Civil War was not kind to Dolores. One day a knock was heard at the door. Her husband and her eldest son were escorted away, never to be seen again. Dolores ploughed on, dressed in mourning from that day on, nurturing the company. Finally, her second son joined her in 1955 and things began to take off in a big way.

Soon the British press began to talk about "The two big houses of Penedès." Prior to that, there had only been one, Codorniú. Dolores died, aged 89, having overseen the emergence of the biggest winemaking empire in Catalonia. When she died, the workers at Freixenet took her body on their shoulders for burial.

Today Freixenet invoices a figure around $380,000,000 annually, exports to all known wine markets and has a storage capacity of 140 million bottles. Much of the world-beating Catalan innovation that has helped shape today's wine industry, took place here. If you visit the bodega today you will see robots moving, storing and packing bottles at an unbelievable rate.

Even Manuel Durán, the corporation's deputy president, has been known to get lost in its enormous, labyrinthine interior. There is a vigour and an unstoppable sense of purpose behind this bodega.

When you look around at the prosperity that winemaking has brought to Penedès you can see the enormous impact that Freixenet has had on the region, for it is their example that so many have succeeded in following. True enough, there has been a healthy rivalry with the other big house, Codorniú, a competition that, if anything, has helped to spur the industry on to reach greater heights.

Conde de Caralt is the label used to market still wines and cava. As you might imagine from such a large and industrious concern, there is always something new to enjoy.

A new barrique-fermented Xarel-lo is a real revelation. It is unctuous and dense in the glass, has a great nose that is deep without being cloying, and a long, lingering after-flavour. Whatever wine you choose, one thing is certain, it will be tremendous value for money.

Visits, as with René Barbier, by appointment.

JOAN VIVES GAU

The drive to Pla de Manlleu is not in the same league as going to Priorato, yet it is still a slow, windy narrow road for 13km from Sant Jaume dels Domenys to Pla de Manlleu. On this road (TP 2442) to the J.V. Gau bodega it is difficult to maintain an average speed of 50km/h along the scrubby limestone ridges devoid of a decent tree; this is tough country.

For 10km, a relatively long way in this region with a village every few kilometres, there would be less than five hectares of arable land. One can not help but wonder why people settled in these remote locations as it must have been an incredibly difficult life before the advent of electricity and the motor car.

Having said that, it is worth the journey just for the pleasure of overlooking El Vendrell, the great Penedès Valley and onto the Mediterranean Sea. Mind you, parking is a considerable problem at the scenic points on this road and one can only advise a trip to the top while surveying stopping points on the way down.

Having reached the tiny village of Pla de Manlleu, it is another job to find the Gau bodega. Continue on the road which is now T 244 to the third track, literally a track, on your right, there will be a large roadside stone with a metal sign saying Can Cendra, that is the key phrase, Can Cendra. That's the signal to turn right and follow the unpaved, rough track uphill until you think you have missed your destination. Not true, keep going until you see on your left, the only Australian flowering eucalyptus within coo-ee and then you are there. Not that there is any sign or directional assistance. In Spain, and its overseas satellites, you are supposed to know where you are going.

You have finally arrived at 500 metres altitude and Mas de la Basserola Also the home of Joan Vives Gau, Mas de la Basserola is the label on the bottles produced here. These tell you that the family has been in business since 1843 and that their main business is cava but they do have four wine labels. The rosada is up there with other good wines from the district, Cupatge Flor with 15% Macabeo is an interesting blend, the Parellada Flor with a touch of sweetness is a popular wine, both whites are 10.5% alcohol. Of special note is that the non-vintage Cabernet Sauvignon, an unusual bottling which did not appear to have been in oak barrels

C.I.G.R.A.V.I.

By Penedès standards Compañia Internacional de Grandes Vinos is a small winery, actually called Finca El Pont, and is partly owned by Remy Cointreau of France. Today it produces mainly cava, but also has still wine in its portfolio. Originally this bodega was dedicated to making brandy, but when brandy stopped selling well about 25 years ago, it was converted to wine and cava production. Today the production is geared to 92% cava and eight percent wine.

There are 50 hectares of vineyards in the Penedès region, some laying fallow prior to re-planting. The three white varieties of Macabeo, Xarel-lo and Parellada are accompanied by Muscat of Alexandria. The wines are, of course, all white and follow the traditional Penedès formula of being base wines for cava, adapted to still wine production. As such they are high in acidity, low in alcohol, pretty firm and probably best accompanied by grilled fish with plenty of lemon juice.

The Giró Ribot Blanc de Blancs, with a production of about 14,000 cases, is a blend of the three local stars and carries 11% by volume of alcohol, a steady performer in the local style. Giro Ribot Muscat is a fruity wine, one of the few of its kind. This wine may be improved with a little better sugar to acid balance. Aromatic grape varieties such as the Muscats are normally more acceptable with a slight touch of sugar. However, this wine does have its own market.

Other labels are the well-known cava brand Paul Chenau - and Masia Parera. Exports go mainly to the USA (a big customer) and Germany.

Visits are available by appointment.

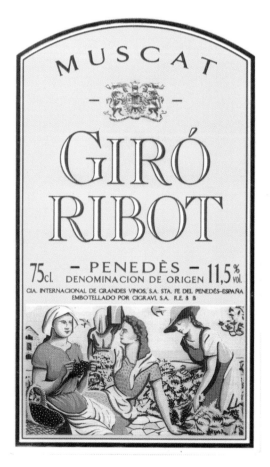

A stunning Merlot Rosé

JORDI LLUCH LLUCH

Although the Lluch family had grown vines for generations, selling their harvest to others, they bought a bodega in 1984 and began to transform it to their own needs. Jordi Lluch, the father, who is still in charge of the vineyards, began the work. His eldest son, also Jordi, is now the oenologist, and younger brother Santi is the commercial manager.

Jordi is solely in charge of oenology in a bodega that is not overly sophisticated, tending more to an artesanal mould. Where this bodega stands out is in having control of 18 - 20 hectares at Cal Escud, two km from the bodega. They have been growing grapes there for about thirty years. In terms of white, these include Macabeo, Xarel-lo and Parellada. The red varieties grown are Cariñena and Merlot, all nearby in the Alt Penedès.

Come harvest time you will see father out harvesting with his tractor and trailer, son busy making wine, and his brother Santi loading the bodega´s new van ready to transport cases of wine to market. The bodega has a total capacity of around 500,000 litres. The vast majority of production is still wine - in good years cava production might reach 20%, no more. The wines are aimed mainly at local sales, with the white van delivering to Sitges and the coastal resort restaurants.

Vinya Escud is the family wine label which includes Blanco and Rosado Joven, Rosada varietal. There are also a tinto Merlot and a Cabernet Sauvignon crianza.

The white wine is a blend of the traditional three grapes of the region, the proportion varying slightly according to the year. The Rosada is made with skin contact extended over 12 hours. Maceration for the tinto is in the region of about 10 to 12 days at 22-24 degrees. It then spends a short period of time in oak casks before passing into bottle, although this is not so easy to detect in the final product.

At the moment, the proportions of wine made at the bodega are almost 50% red, 20% rosé and 30% white. There is an increasing demand for tintos, and Merlot certainly seems to be the way forward for this bodega.

Vinya Escud Merlot Rosada has an intense, red-pink colour containing plenty of fruit aroma. Prunes, plums, some watermelon and dried peach come to mind and in the mouth it is quite powerful. You could easily see this wine as an accompaniment to food, say a chicken dish. Vinya Escud Merlot tinto, is a wine that tends to a more mellow, more oxidised fruit style. It is not as convincing a product as the rosé.

The family still keeps alive the ancient tradition of making *rancio*, or heavily oxidised wines. Demand for this style has dwindled in Catalonia, although across the French border centred around Perpignan, it is very much alive and well. Another tradition kept alive here is the sale of bulk wine at the door for locals, as well as tourist traffic. People who prefer to buy wine from a producer rather than a supermarket find it very satisfying to drive up to a winery and load fresh wine into their own containers.

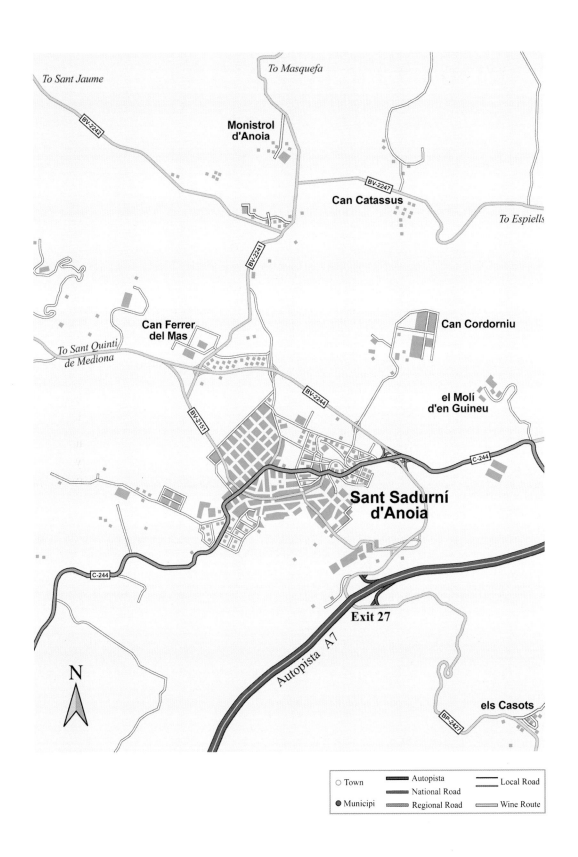

To Sant Jaume

BV-2242

Monistrol d'Anoia

To Masquefa

BV-2247

Can Catassus

To Espiells

BV-2241

Can Ferrer del Mas

To Sant Quinti de Mediona

Can Cordorniu

BV-2244

el Molí d'en Guineu

BV-2151

C-244

Sant Sadurní d'Anoia

C-244

Exit 27

N

Autopista A7

els Casots

BP-2427

○ Town	▬ Autopista		▬ Local Road
	▬ National Road		
● Municipi	▬ Regional Road		▬ Wine Route

SANT SADURNÍ D'ANOIA
Route #5

Includes: Greater Sant Sadurní d'Anoia and three nearby towns. **Scenic spots**: There are claims that Sant Sadurní was discovered by Noah, hence an Ark on the town's crest. Many get a laugh from this claim. The best way to see the town is on foot; find a car park and visit the many cavas or sites. However, you will need a car to visit the biggest players.

Directions: There are two routes to Sant Sadurni from Vilafranca, the direct route on route C243 is the shortest but not recommended as it will be under construction for at least two years and is home to many learner-drivers. The longer, but quicker and more scenic route is via N340, 11 km from Vilafranca to Petrenor service station, turn left on BP2427 winding your way up to the stunning view from el Casots, probably the best panorama in the comarca (county). On the viewer's right is a striking new celler and further distant is the 10th century castle of Subirats. The panoramic view embraces Montserrat in the distance, in the forground is a bird's eye view of the Sant Sadurní township. The sweeping view to the west and south shows exactly how the valley is formed with clearly defined mountains on either side and a series of undulating hills from top (north) to bottom of the valley.

Descending the hill gives the choice of entering the town of Sant Sadurní from the south or by-passing it and visiting cellars on the north side. As the two Cava giants (they don't make table wines under those labels), Freixenet and Codorniu, are not included on our list, it would be very unwise not to visit them both - they are very visible.

Wineries: Phone ahead for appointments

els Casots-Subirats 08739	***B4***
*Pere Llopart Vilaros	93 899 3125
Finca Castell de Subirats	93 899 5329
Moli Coloma	93 891 1092
J. M. Rosell Mir	93 891 1354
Sant Sadurni d'Anoia 08770	***A3***
Agus SA	93 891 0780
Agustí Torello	93 891 1173
Antoni Vilamajor Saumell	93 818 3313
Arvicaretey	93 818 3590
Berral i Miró	93 891 2763
Can Quetu	93 891 1214
Canals Munne	93 891 0318
Carme Guasch Sabaté	93 891 0914
Castel de Vilarnau	93 891 2361
Cavas Lavernoya	93 891 2202
Civica	93 891 2955
Coll de Juny	93 891 0800
*Covides	93 817 2552
Civino	93 891 0300
Durmat	93 891 0734
*Espumosos Del Cava	93 818 3286
Felix Torné Caldú	93891 2132

*Gramona	93 891 0113
Grupo Familia Ventura	93 891 0352
Jaume Giró Giró	93 891 0165
*Joan Raventos Rosell	93 772 5251
*Josep M Raventós Blanch	93 818 3262
J. J. Siguenza Gazguiez	93 775 5216
*Juve i Camps	93 891 1000
Maria del Carme Albesa	93 891 1390
Mata Casanovas	93 891 0214
Mata Portabella	93 891 2552
Nuria Poch Urpi	93 891 0957
Pere Munné Duran	93 786 0148
Ramon Canals Canals	93 775 5446
Ricardo Martinez de Simon	93 891 2775
Robert J. Mur	93 891 0066
Sabaté i Coca	93 891 1927
S.de M.Montserrat Carcasona	93 891 0352
Espiells	***A4***
*El Cep/L'Alzinar	93 891 2353
Monistrol d' Anoia	***A3***
*Marquése de Monistrol	93 891 0276

Restaurants: At els Casots overlooking the northern Penedès Valley is Mirador de les Caves 93 899 3178.

Everything about Juvé y Camps is big and impressive.

Everything

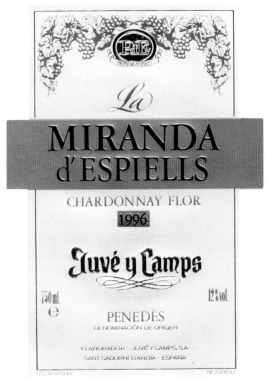

120

JUVE I CAMPS

Established in 1921, Juvé y Camps is a marriage of two families who have succeeded in making one happy family. If there is one dominant building in the cava capital of Sant Sadurni d'Anoia, it is the semi-circular head office and bodega of this company - portrayed on the facing page. Their family masia on the outskirts of St Llorenç d'Hortons is also an impressive edifice and farm.

Juvé y Camps has an enormous 450ha of vineyards divided between nearby Espiells which is planted with the three local favourite white grapes Macabeo, Xarel-lo and Parellada - and further away in the high grounds of Mediona, where Parellada and Cabernet Sauvignon are grown.

These are bolstered by plantings of Chardonnay, Gewurztraminer and Pinot noir. The Pinot noir is currently being used in the firm's Rosé Cava but plans are in hand to produce a still wine from Pinot grapes. Family members are responsible for both the vineyards and the winemaking process. Unusual for such a large firm, Juvé y Camps has never purchased a litre of wine - and all grapes come from their own extensive vineyards

The main bodega located in the centre of the Espiells vineyard, has more than 3,000 barricas for ageing red wines and storage capacity for two million litres in stainless steel. Total production runs at 180,000 cases of wine annually and the sales of the highest quality sparkling cava exceed those of all French producers in Spain.

Casa Vella D'Espiells is the name given to their front line Reserva Cabernet Sauvignon which goes into bottle with about 12% alcohol and a fresh 4.68 grams per litre of acid following ageing in both American and French oak barrels for 12 months. The wine has a further three years in bottle to highlight the predominately black currant flavours and rich red colour. We also noted some cigar box aromas from the time spent in oak.

1993 was the first vintage of Reserva Chardonnay *La Miranda d'Espiells* which spends at least six months in new American oak casks prior to a further year in bottle before release. The Chardonnay fruit comes from Espiells, an area quickly becoming prominent for Chardonnay grapes. This 11% alcohol wine shows good yellow-gold colours and is made from only free-run juice - no pressed wine is added. It is recommended that Chardonnay be served at a comfortable 7-8 degrees Celsius. The name La Miranda comes from a high look-out tower located on the Espiells vineyard.

Juvé y Camps have thriving export markets in the USA, Germany, Japan, UK, Venezuela and Switzerland.

Visits can be arranged by appointment although the firm has no sales facilities for visitors.

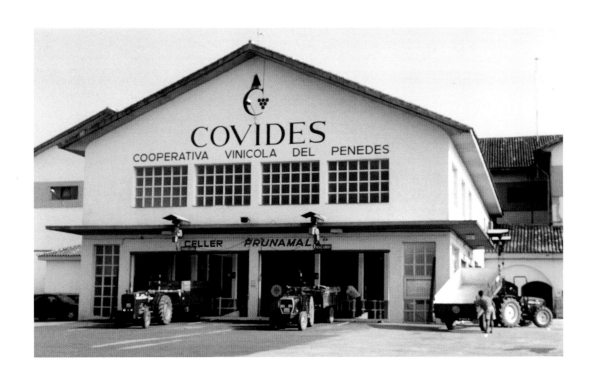

Author's Choice

Cabernet Rosé

COVIDES

With 800 members located in 32 Penedès towns who control 3,000 hectares of grapes, Covides is the most important and certainly the most modern co-operative in Catalonia. Not that this is one bodega, rather there are three winery sites in the Penedès region. The principal one in both the co-op's eyes and those of the visitor is just a kilometre or so south west of Sant Sadurni on the road to Vilafranca. Other processing facilities are located at Sant Marti Sarroca and Sant Cugat Sesgarrigues while the head office is located on Avenue Tarragona, Vilafranca del Penedès.

Covides processes an impressive 30 million litres (about 50/50 wine and cava) annually and this is elevated to award-winning cavas and wines in a number of different labels. The top label is the Duc de Foix range which includes a Red Reserva made with Cabernet and Tempranillo, a Crianza and a varietal Cabernet Sauvignon among the reds. There is also a rosé, while the white range includes a Chardonnay, a traditional white from the local big three grapes, then varietal wines made from each of Macabeo, Xarel-lo and Parellada.

There is no doubt that chief oenologist Emili Esteve and his crew are very comfortable with making red wines; they do that well and it is a pity that only 10% of production is dedicated to red wines as many think this is the future for Penedès producers, and certainly with their Asian customers.

The cava base wines are excellent but this wine making philosophy is carried over to the white wines and may require re-thinking as the company extends its overseas markets. The claim is that Covides' clients in the UK want relatively low alcohol (11%) wines. This is also a desirable level of alcohol for cava base wine. Even the Chardonnay at 12% alcohol misses the ripe fruit flavours that this variety can give at increased ripening levels. The 100% Cabernet rosé is a wonderful food wine.

There is a mid range known as Moli de Foc which is selling well in the Scandanavian countries, Germany, France and Holland includes a Tempranillo red and rosé, dry and semi-sweet whites made from the big three Macabeo, Xarel-lo and Parellada.

The supermarket range runs under the Xenius label and includes a Blanco dry and semi-sweet, a Tempranillo Rose and red. Of course, cava wines are included in all ranges and it is of interest that the Xenius cava picked up a gold medal in a far distant Florida, USA wine competition! All the cooperative wines enjoy the approval for DO Penedès, as do the cava wines which are approved by DO Cava.

The visitor can drive-in and purchase wine (fresh fruit, vegetables in season and a selection of nuts are also available) weekdays from 0800-1300 and 1500-1800. However, for a tour of the plant, bookings must be made by phone.

Coop El Cep

L'Alzinar, Marques de Gelida

To reach this somewhat isolated bodega, take the Sant Sadurni - Masquefa road BV2241 and two km from Sant Sadurni you will come to a river crossing, turn right at signs for Can Catassus and Espiells (BV2247), proceed past the impressive school of viticulture, turn left on dirt road at big metal L'Alzinar/Marqués de Gelida sign and follow to Coop El Cep.

People in these parts do not deliberately try to confuse visitors, but because few bodegas encourage visitors, some confusion about names does happen. Many establishments have a profusion of names, none more than this one. The business name is Vins El Cep SA, according to the owners, but officially they are Cooperativ El Cep, albeit a co-operative of very few people. This is not a cooperative belonging to a district or a large number of members.

To make things more difficult for the casual acquaintance, the labels are far better known than the company name. L'Alzinar, with its very good wines, is a prominent label; Marqués de Gelida is not quite as visible.

The winery is a basic bodega, not gleaming with hi-tech toys, but the woman's touch is evident in the production department by excellent packaging and attractive labels designed for this age. Maite Esteve is a talented and competent manager who has a business economics degree from Barcelona University (photo on page 44).

This is a sizable operation with 200 ha of diverse vineyards - some around the bodega with splendid views down the Penedès Valley - more in the upper locations of Sant Lorenç d'Hortons and Gelida. Still wine production of nearly 10,000 cases includes a very good Chardonnay - among the best in the region - an equally good Tempranillo, and the traditional Blanc de Blancs.

Nearly 25,000 cases of cava are made by this firm who look to increase their range of still wine varietals, including a reserva negre, in the future. Currently wines are exported to the USA and Germany.

Visits by appointment.

Espumosos del Cava

Blancher

Espumosos is located in the downtown area of Sant Sadurni d'Anoia on main road C244 in the direction of Gelida. When walking or driving around this thriving town it is hard to understand that almost the entire town sits on top of a labyrinth of underground wine cellars. Espumosos, for example, has three stories beneath ground level where the wine and cava production takes place. Some others go down six to seven floors.

The ground floor is devoted to a sales area, reception and offices. First floor down is the cellar and winemaking areas, next floor down is devoted mainly to red wine production while the third floor is wholly devoted to wine-in-barrel storage.

Like so many other producers on Route #5, Espumosos has a profusion of names known only to locals (like El Cep on facing page); everyone knows Blancher - but not when they are looking for Espumosos de Cava!

Espumosos del Cava was established in 1955 by the Capdevila Blancher family who appear to have spent all their efforts in this building rather than in vineyards. Their vineyards total only 10 hectares - a very small holding by local standards. However, the Penedès region is served by 5,800 grape growers while there are only 138 wineries, so there is little need for every bodega to be a grape grower. The firm is now managed by the Carbó Planas family.

There are three still wine labels - white and rosé, both of 11% alcohol and negre (red) with 12.5% alcohol. This would indicate that the red is made as a true still wine whereas the other two are the standard cava base wines. In addition to the Catalan and national Spanish markets, Blancher wines are also on sale in the UK

One section of the bodega has been set aside as a museum which is open for inspection week days from 0830-1300 and again from 1500-1830. Weekend and holiday hours are 0900-1400.

The future of Gramona - like so many other bodegas - is in the hands of nieces & nephews.

Gessami

GRAMONA

Javier and Jacques Gramona are cousins with a single, fixed idea: to make exceptional wines. The building where their bodega is situated was built in 1881 by their great-grandfather and winemaking has been a family tradition for 200 years. As generations have married, acquired and lost land and property, their vineyards have spread around the neighbouring countryside. One advantage to come out of this is that different *terroir* has become available to them, and they have not been slow to take advantage of it.

The only inheritance from the past that restricts them somewhat is that, because at one stage wealthier families preferred to have their cellars in town, their current bodega is now hemmed in by buildings on all sides, right in the middle of town. Their success also means that the 40 hectares of their own vineyards have to be bolstered by grapes bought from another 20 hectares to which they have access. "Parellada grows better in the hills than in the lowlands," says Javier. They buy-in Gewurztraminer, Sauvignon (blanc) and Riesling grapes.

From the wine lover's point of view it is what the modern generation is doing that is of most interest. Jacques is in charge of Ph.D. studies at the University of Tarragona, School of Oenology. This places him in an enviable position. Not only are the latest thoughts on hygiene and winemaking incorporated into daily practice, he also has access to some important benefits.

First, the bodega has been able to use advanced technology to isolate and then propagate their own natural yeasts, from the grapes in their own vineyards. These yeasts can impart to wines their special flavours unique to the varieties they use. So as to filter out any rogue strains that might develop over the years, they control all changes in the yeasts' phenotype fingerprints. To achieve this, they utilise a tagging system based on Carbon 14 traces. A five year agreement between the faculty and the bodega enables them to do this work. Another great deal is that there are three university students working at the bodega. One covers the demands imposed by belonging to the ISO 9002 protocols, one covers QC, or quality control, and the other assists Jacques with general oenology. This means that, including Javier's father, there are no less than five post-graduate oenologists working within the confines of a small bodega.

The Gramona Gran Cru Chardonnay is a mouth-filling wine, clearly able to age well in bottle. Perhaps the most curious and outstanding wine is called Gessamí. It is made from 50% Sauvignon (blanc), 40% Muscat and 10% Gewurztraminer. The grapes are left on the vine to super-mature until they reach a potential of 14-18% alcohol. Then a process of cryo-extraction is used, by freezing the must. At this stage what is called super-extraction is brought into operation. There is a small part of the must that does not freeze. This is removed to a vat and fermented at between 14° -16° C using a cryogenic yeast. When the wine reaches 140-150 grams of sugar and 9.5% alcohol it is suddenly chilled to 10° C, protecting the colloidal content. The final result really is quite special.

The on-site wine store is open daily for sales and cellar visits are available by appointment.

"Today, the small settlement with a winery within its own village, is a unique and fascinating place to live and work".

MARQUÉS DE MONISTROL

In the valley of Monistrol d'Anoia, within a landscape that has changed little over the centuries, you will find one of the oldest links with wine's past, the bodegas of Marqués de Monistrol. Documents dating back to the 9th and 10th centuries describe how a small monastery was established on this site, and cared for by friars, one of whose main tasks was the cultivation of vines and, of course, the making of wine.

Some 150 years later the property passed into the hands of feudal landlords, thus forming the Marquisette of Monistrol, from which the current bodega takes its name. The Marqués of Monistrol inherited from the church, and in 1882, from his ancestors 450 hectares that take up the whole of the sub-valley of the Anoia River in Monistrol d'Anoia in the municipi of Sant Sadurni d'Anoia, a mere 38 km from the great city of Barcelona.

Today the small settlement with a winery within its own village, is a unique and fascinating place to live and work. In 1999 all the vineyard land was sold by the Marqués to other interests.

Over the ages the bodega has dedicated itself to producing the different styles of wine fashionable at the time. Some early wines were thick and *licorosos* (syrup-like), then at the end of the 18th century to the beginning of the 19th century, brandy distilling was practised. Finally, towards the beginning of this century cava made its appearance at Monistrol.

As production director, Antonio Olivé Martí explains that today Chardonnay, Macabeo, Xarel-lo and Parellada are the white grapes grown, and Cabernet Sauvignon, Garnacha, Merlot, Monastrell, Pinot noir and Tempranillo make up the red plantings. New plantings of Cabernet Franc and Syrah should begin to produce early this century.

Currently the winery has a capacity of 5.5 million litres of storage plus 2,000 American oak 225 litre barrels for maturation of the red wines. The winery is almost equally devoted to still wines and cava.

Good value for money is one of the strong points of the wines from Monistrol who bottle every wine in their own branded bottle. Their barrel fermented Chardonnays have good varietal character and are well structured. Tempranillo (60%, with grapes bought in) and Cabernet Sauvignon blend has just the right touch of American oak and when selling retail in the UK at the end of 1999 for £3.49 represents excellent value. For restaurants in Spain you can look for the special Masia Monistrol label.

Merlot, all from own vineyards, at 50 pence more is an equally attractive proposition, as is the Cabernet. Slightly higher up the scale is the Reserva Privada, a very nice combination of Cabernet Sauvignon and Tempranillo.

The label is owned by the Spanish drinks giant, Madrid-based Arco group, who also own the Martins winery in Argentina. Arco are very professional marketers and Marqués de Monistrol products are available in over 30 countries around the world.

Visits by appointment only.

MASIA MONISTROL
Tempranillo Garnacha
1998
PENEDÈS
DENOMINACION DE ORIGEN

MARQUES DE MONISTROL
— RESERVA DE L'HEREU —
1996

FUNDADA EN 1882
MONISTROL D'ANOIA

SERIE LIMITADA

PENEDÈS
DENOMINACION DE ORIGEN

MARQUES DE MONISTROL
— DESDE 1882 —
MACABEO-PARELLADA
1998
PENEDÈS
DENOMINACION DE ORIGEN

PERE LLOPART VILAROS

As mentioned on page 117, the alternative route to Sant Sadurni d'Anoia is via road BP2427 which will bring you to Llopart Cava and Bodegas. Should you visit these wine routes and only take this one, you will not be disappointed. They have an absolute stunning view, probably one of five best in the wine world. The visitor cannot help but think that only good wines can be made in such a place, and that is correct.

The aspect looks over the town of Sant Sadurni d'Anoia, north Penedès Valley and Montserrat - further up the road there is the old 10th century Subirat castle and it does appears as though, when building new cellars, the family took heed of the past, as the new premises are something in the way of a modern fortress. You will not get in here without having a massive gate opened by remote control.

However, as modern as it is, there is real history manifested here as the original cellar dates back to 1330 and the Llopart family have lived in this house for seven centuries. Fortunately the family have, with considerable pride, amply documented the facts.

Although, once again, the bias is 80% towards cava production, Llopart makes very good wine. A barrel fermented Chardonnay would be among the four or five best of Penedès. It is a classic demonstration of the marriage benefits of fruit, oak and malo-lactic (secondary) fermentation. In one of the many evaluations made of Catalan wines, this was the top wine.

The name Llopart pops up fairly often in these parts, as can be seen on page 143 another family making excellent wines not far away in Gelida trades under the name of Torello Llopart. The els Casots family is Pere Llopart

The firm has carefully laid plans for the introduction of red wines, Reserva only reds will come onto the market in 2005 - and they will be made only in years of excellence. Certainly a label not to be missed.

Open weekends - visiting hours are 1030-1400; other times by appointment only.

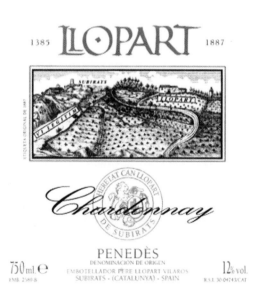

The old oak tree, source of so much tradition.

El Preludi

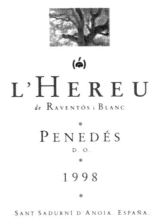

L'HEREU
de RAVENTÓS i BLANC

•

PENEDÉS
D.O.

•

1998

•

SANT SADURNÍ D'ANOIA. ESPAÑA.

75 cl.

ELABORADOR
JOSEP MARIA RAVENTÓS i BLANC, S.A
R.G.E. 1115 B   R.S.I. 30 4481 CAT

11 % VOL

RAVENTOS I BLANC

Raventós i Blanc is located in the Place of the Oak, right opposite the giant Codorníu complex, in the settlement of Can Codorníu - and there lies a number of interesting stories.

The first story concerns a 1986 family separation from the Raventós family, owners of Codorníu, the founders of cava and one of the world's largest sparkling wine producers. Josep Maria Raventós held a key executive position in the family operation but for reasons best known to himself, he went over the road in the shade of the giant oak and built one of Spain's finest and most novel bodegas.

Just driving into the car park you realize that this is a Fortune 500 company; the architecture is unostentatious - but screams big money, class and forward thinking. In fact, two of Spain's most notable architects, Gabriel Mora and Jaume Bach, were responsible for this very sensitive building which blends superbly into its location. From the inside there are quite stunning views of the gardens and the mighty century old oak tree which is the company's logo and guardian.

However, while elegance and architecture are commendable and signals a good impression of company philosophy, wineries are about making wine and this Raventós i Blanc do very well.

Raventós i Blanc has its own 88 hectares of vineyards located around the Alt Penedès, each vineyard offers its best to a specific variety. La Plana and El Maiol de Forment fincas (farms) for Xarel-lo, El Prat vineyard supplies Macabeo,

La Barbera for Parellada, the Chardonnay comes from La Vinya Gran, while Xarel-lo, Macabeo and Parellada are sourced from El Serral de la Rigola.

Winemakers Josep Maria Raventós and Joaña Viñas (pictured on page 44), craft wines with exotic names such as El Preludi, a blend of the three traditional varieties plus Chardonnay which the company genuinely admits is a cava base - and l'Hereu (the first son of the family). l'Hereu is a blend of 15% Cabernet Sauvignon, 80% Tempranillo and 5% Merlot with 11.5% alcohol. This is an unusual, relatively low alcohol style, yet the company rightly considers it a traditional Penedès wine. El Preludi (the beginning) is dry wine containing a slight sparkle to help preserve the richness of its aromas.

There is an unoaked Chardonnay of 12% alcohol level, made in stainless steel and showing all the life and freshness of this variety.

The Raventós i Blanc products, which wear imposing labels, are exported to Austria, Switzerland and the UK. The company encourages visitors to its imposing premises Monday-Thursday 0900-1200 again from 1500-1700; Fridays 0900-1200.

Best phone beforehand for an appointment.

133

PENEDÈS VALLEY NORTH

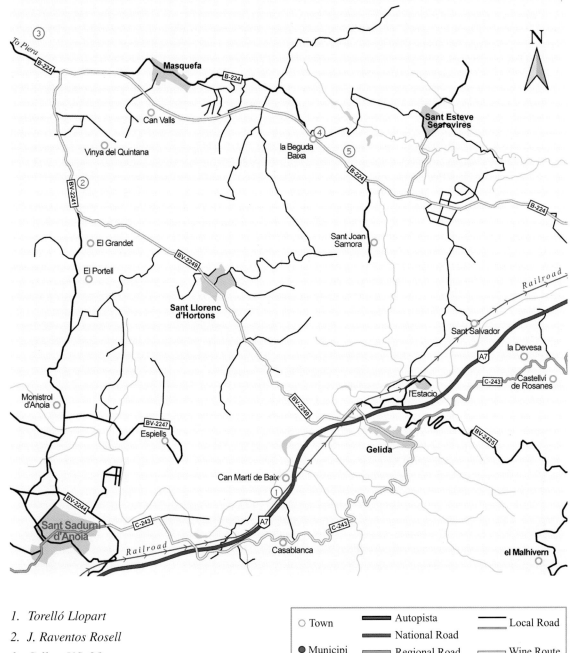

1. Torelló Llopart
2. J. Raventos Rosell
3. Cellers V.S. 96
4. Castell d'Age
5. Masia Bach

○ Town	▬ Autopista		▬ Local Road
	▬ National Road		
● Municipi	▬ Regional Road		▬ Wine Route

PENEDÈS VALLEY NORTH
ROUTE #6

Includes: Gelida, Sant Llorenç d'Hortons, Masquefa, St Esteve ses Rovires. (A visit to Piera is recommended).

Scenic spots: Gelida, crossroads of a river, railway, freeway and the ancient Via Augusta; Castle of Gelida dates to 945AD. Something to ponder while driving through Masquefa is that the Count of Barcelona sold his 10th century Masquefa castle for a 1,000 salaries! Superb views of Montserrat are seen along this route, particularly from Masquefa and Can Bonastere.

St Esteve ses Rovires boasts probably the best life-style in Alt Penedès, with splendid sporting and service facilities, wildlife and one excellent winery.

Gelida 08790	*A4*		*St Esteve ses Rovires*	*A4*
Bodegas Montcau	93 779 0034		*Masia Bach	93 771 4052
*Torelló Llopart	93 891 0793			
Sant Llorenç d'Hortons 08791 A4			*Not on map*	
J. Carreras A	93 771 6251		Masia Freixe (Piera)	93 776 2528
Josep Almuzara Carreras	93 771 6079		Ramon Canals Canals	93 775 2528
*Castell d'Age	93 772 5181			
Masquefa 08783	*A4*			
*J. Raventos Rosell	93 891 0030			
*Cellers V.S. 96	93 772 5283			

Due to haze and smog Monserrat (serrated mountain), the Catalan icon,
is probably the autonomia's most difficult photographic subject.

Above - typical country around Castell d'Age. Olive trees, vines and Montserrat.

Below - Ann-Marie Junyent standing at the doorway of her bodega.

Negre

CASTEL D'AGE

Swiss-born Anne-Marie Junyent is a charming, magnetic and talented person. Mother, company president, oenologist and ecologist, she, along with her husband Josep, is quietly changing the way a few things are done in the Catalan wine industry. Yet, judging by the shop front of their Castell d'Age cellars, one could be excused for thinking that this is some small-town hick operation.

The town has a total of 10 buildings facing the main road from Masquefa to Martorell, in the small village of La Beguda Baixa (there's a La Beguda Alt just up the road). It is hard to conceive that behind the largest, and probably the most feeble looking building is a dynamic wine operation going places quickly. Anne-Marie will fret about this facade until the budget priority says time to renovate.

From her four wheel drive vehicle, which was the only way of traversing the deluged site, Ann Marie proudly showed-off the couple's 120 hectares of vines which she claims are Catalonia's best.

Large mounds of pungent animal manure, used as natural fertilizer, are dotted around the vineyard. Ann-Marie's Swiss upbringing taught her to respect the land and its people. The philosophy is to use a bicycle or walk rather than a vehicle, eat natural foods and snack on fruit rather than packaged junk food.

However, to harvest their large vineyard holdings the couple have purchased several machine harvesters which are used for 80 percent of the crop - an inevitable concession to the future.

Many winelovers think that ecological wines, or any of those other kinky names are not normal. No, these are not only good wines, they are very good wines, produced showing a caring for the land that produces them.

The agricultural ecologica Blanc is in the style of most cava base wines, 11% alcohol, fresh with acid but this wine carries a lot more flavour than wines going into bubbly. Unusual for this region, the major partner in the blend is Chenin (blanc) accompanied by Xarello which provides a fresh pineapple aroma that jumps up to meet you.

The Castel d'Age Negre, made from Cabernet and Tempranillo, is among the front rank of Penedes reds. My notes say "good sweet fruit, good tannins, mouth-filling and clean finish - I like!" It was judged along with other rather heavyweight regional wines and stood up to them all.

Other labels are Chenier, Vilademany, Alexandra and Ann-Marie Comtés.

The on-site retail shop is open weekdays 0800-1300 and weekends 1000-1400 for wine sales.

A bodega with a view!

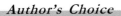

Author's Choice

Merlot

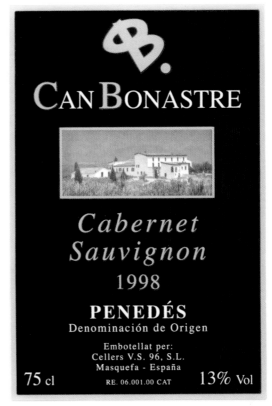

Cellars VS96

Can Bonastre

This bodega's rather curious name stems from the fact that señor Vallés married a señorita named Salvany, hence the family name is Vallés Salvany. The wine company was set up in 1996 to sell its own bottled wine. "You can go crazy searching for a name," says Martín Vallés. "We must have looked at hundreds. Finally we decided on something simple."

Simple or not, it is a name worth remembering, for the wines are very good indeed. Bear in mind that this bodega sells its wines under the label, Can Bonastre, which is the name of the handsome farmhouse that is home to the bodega. The house is situated on a great vantage point where you can view its surrounding vineyards.

Martín Valles' father purchased the land in 1986. As the second son of a traditional Catalan farming family he had missed out on the inheritance of the family holding. Throughout his working life he harboured a desire to own an estate in Penedès. Eventually he was able to do this, although he died before being able to really enjoy his acquisition. His son, also called Martín, a chemist by profession, took the oenology course at Barcelona University and is now the oenological lynchpin of the bodega. His own son, Roger, has forsaken the television industry to look after the wine marketing.

To begin with the family sold all the grapes harvested to other wine makers. Then in 1993 the price of grapes dropped to such a point that it was felt prudent to make wine instead. First this was done in a hired plant as the new winery was slowly set up. As a consequence, the oldest piece of equipment you will see dates from 1994. New stainless steel, new presses, new refrigeration equipment, and a new and forward-thinking winemaking approach all give this bodega a positive feel.

Can Bonastre Sauvignon (blanc) is a wine born out of an attempt to select the most appropriate Sauvignon clone for local conditions. There is varietal quality, length and depth about the chosen clone.

Pinot noir has also come out with great expression. The first harvests were destined to rosé as Martín was afraid that a lack of colour and low maturity would make a red wine difficult to sell. The rosé, is quite deep in colour, while the first reds are more than intriguing.

Only still wine is made at Can Bonastre. The line up includes: Chardonnay, Pinot noir, Merlot, Cabernet Sauvignon as young wine and crianza, annual production is increasing from 4,000 cases in 1998 leading to a full production of the vineyard's total harvest capacity.

Can Bonastre Chardonnay shows good colour extraction. The wine has not been in oak barrels, has quite a focussed aroma and good fruit character. In the mouth the wine has great flavour, good structure with a citrus quality.

Merlot is also a pure varietal, all with a future ahead which normally has six months in wood. Cabernet Sauvignon wines have very dark colour and a good mouthful of pure fruit; a very good wine.

Cabernet Sauvignon crianza again has a very dark colour, with all the good characters of the above wine.

No longer in disrepair, Masia Bach is now a showpiece.

Author's Choice

Tempranillo

MASIA BACH

Two brothers, Pere and Ramón Bach, were textile merchants of some note, with important cotton factories in Barcelona around the beginning of the century. With no heirs to take over from them, the property was eventually sold to the Mata family, also textile barons. In 1967 the property passed into the ownership of the Rockefeller Group and finally, in 1975 the major cava producer, Codorníu, bought the label and company. By this stage the old Masia Bach had fallen into disrepair and most of its vineyards sold.

Codorníu greatly expanded and modernised the bodega and draw grapes from 100 suppliers. Today you see continuous band presses receiving white grapes, the red wine grapes coming in through a separate entry. There are two kilometres of excavated caves on the property, holding mainly American oak barrels. All the red wines of Masia Bach pass through oak barrels. Extrísimo blanco, a white wine, also goes through some oak treatment. As a point of interest, Extrísimo is the name given to very high quality cotton.

Capacity at Masia Bach has grown tremendously to a point where there are approximately six million litres of stainless steel, a similar amount to the annual wine sales. Notwithstanding this, major expansion plans are afoot.

Among the white wines, Extrisimo Seco is made from Xarel-lo, Macabeo and Chardonnay. It is not made as base wine for cava. The idea is to aim for a mature wine style, led by the Xarel-lo, a splendid idea. It should be drunk young, but will last quite happily over a year. It is not put through a malolactic fermentation, so it retains a nice crisp level of acidity.

The 100% Chardonnay equivalent contains 15% of barrel fermented wine and sells out very quickly.

Viña Extrísima is a blend of Tempranillo, Cabernet, Pinot, Merlot and Garnacha. This unusual combination gives a pleasing style aided by nine months in oak which lends a warm aroma and bouquet with plenty of ripe fruit underneath. Bach Tempranillo has good, deep colour and a delicate hint of wood makes this pure Tempranillo stand out well. For a Tempranillo, it is big in the mouth, with a tannic level that gives it plenty of space.

The Masia Bach Cabernet Sauvignon contains 85% Cabernet and 15% Tempranillo. This deep coloured wine spends 12 months in oak and has loads of dark, tree fruit (plums and cherries) flavours, also with a nuance of capsicum and cassis on the nose. It is an aromatic wine with a long and persistent finish.

The team behind each wine includes technical director Miguel Gurpide, who also directs work at Codorníu's other winery at Raimat in Lérida, along with Jordi Botta, the local oenologist.

In a complete turn-around from when the textile brothers started the bodega, Masia Bach could now be classed as a woman's winery. The expansive big chief of Codorníu is a lady who relies on other women in important roles.

Bach accepts visitors, preferably by appointment but does make an unusual 200 pesatas charge for sampling their wines.

Above - the main entrance with a magnificent view towards Montserrat.

Blanc Tranquille

Left - Antonio, the youngest of the Torelló clan, in the family cellars.

142

TORELLÓ LLOPART

To continue a remarkable scenic tour of the northern Penedès Valley, take the C243 road on Route 6 from Sant Sadurni d'Anoia. Follow the windy road for six kilometres to the small village of Casablanca which is half way between St Sadurni and Gelida, then turn left at the well-marked gate sign - Can Marti de Baix.

Right from the front gate you become aware that this is a class operation, Proceed a further two km along their own concrete road and if you cross the autopista and railway line, you know you are on the right road!

Firstly you will overlook the masia and vineyards, then arrive at the home and cellars of the 24th Llopart generation who are now in charge of this 600 year old house. Yes, you have opened a page of history.

Torelló Llopart are rightly famous for their superb cava products which have appeared on the dining tables of many famous European celebrities. The high note was when Torelló Llopart was selected as *the* bubbly for the 2,000 VIPs who attended the Barcelona concert of the three great tenors - José Carreras, Plácido Domingo and Luciano Pavarotti. In fact, eldest son and oenologist, Francisco is a common sight at major functions in Spain and other countries.

While cava is still the backbone of the Torelló family bodega, a still white wine made from the big three local whites, Macabeo, Xarel-lo and Parrelada is a hot seller. Low in alcohol at 10.5% it is still a clean and fresh dry white that goes well with the seafood so abundant in these parts. A Cabernet and Merlot blended red wine will grace the wine store shelves in 2001, and taking into account the quality of the family's other products, this will surely be a winner.

The present day company is vigorously headed by Sra. Ernestina Torelló Llopart, a striking mother of the other two principals, sons oenologist Francisco, and Antonio, who attends to public relations and marketing,

Torelló Llopart products are widely available in Spain and exports are around 16-20%, mainly to Japan. With 110 hectares of vines surrounding Can Marti de Baix the company is well poised to meet their future desires of the highest quality produced from their own grapes.

J. Raventós Rosell

Although the owner's name is Raventós Rosell, the name given to the property is Heretat Vall-Ventós, a union between the wife's name (Vallverdu) and Raventós. The surname is well known in the region, but is not connected to other wine-making eponyms.

The venture's first harvest came in 1990, drawn from 60 hectares surrounding the winery and 30 ha around Sant Sadurni. Today, more and more vines are being planted, with large tracts around the house being prepared for red grapes.

From the very outset, Joan Raventós opted for outright quality. He asked his winemaker, Josep Maria Sempere, to design the operation with this sole aim in mind. Delighted, Josep Maria determined that yields should be held low and that hygiene had to be kept to a maximum. What is even more remarkable is that wine prices are also kept reasonably low, making these wines a real find.

The house itself is old. A tile bearing the date 1700 was found from another home, at the base of a sundial, dating from 1726. Sundials were usually set up when all the work on a house was complete.

The 100% Chardonnay has a lovely deep yellow colour, some hints of green, 12.5% alcohol, getting up there with the ripe fruit with an enormous and very impressive nose. Many would consider this wine as a splenid example of a Chardonnay varietal.

Sauvignon (blanc) is again charged with plenty of colour. Oenologist Josep Maria insists that in order to make wine he opts for best maturity first, and colour subsequently if needs be. The nose is quite full in the face gooseberry, with some wild herbs and small amounts of asparagus dominate the aroma of this wine. The winemaker says the Sauvignon has good balance and it reminds him of the Mediterranean.

Chenin (blanc) is a little lighter in colour and less dense-looking in glass. Not being an aromatic variety as is Sauvignon, the Chenin is not as powerful but it is very well made. This wine is an ideal accompaniment to sea food.

Pinot noir, actually a blanc de noir, cannot be sold as such because it has confused the Consejo Regulador - so it is sold as a Pinot noir. It is however a tremendous white wine with a fascinating nose and flavour.

THE RAVAGES OF HAIL!

Summer Hail

Similar vine before

Vines After

Spring Hail

A donkey cart and owner, bush vines and olive trees living happily together.

Below - the bulldozer sculpted, awesome, terraces hang precariously to a hillside.

PRIORATO
THE OLD & THE NEW

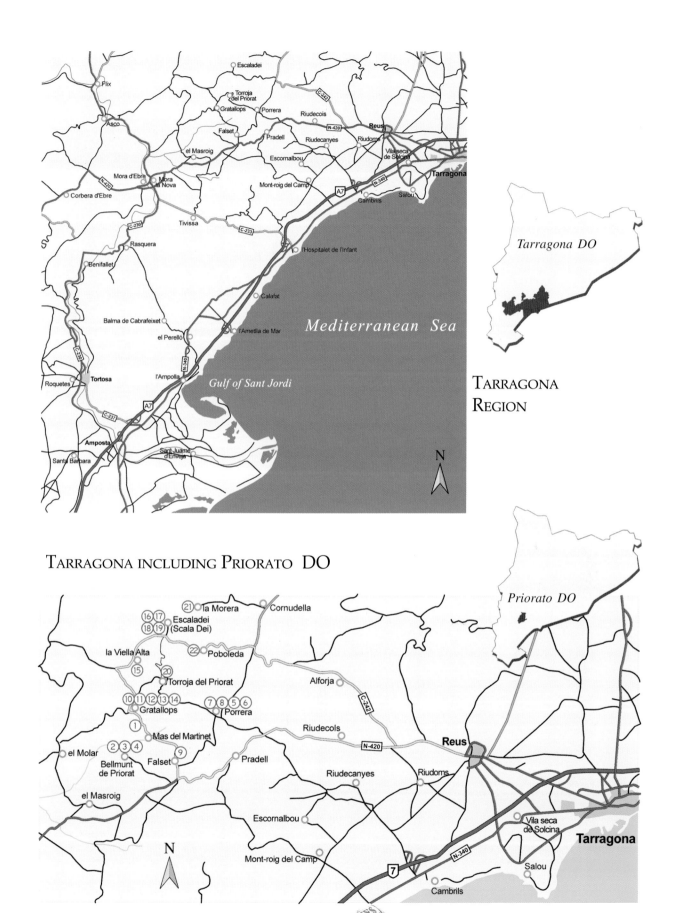

Tarragona DO

TARRAGONA REGION

Mediterranean Sea

Gulf of Sant Jordi

N

TARRAGONA INCLUDING PRIORATO DO

Priorato DO

N

1. MAS MARTINET VITICULTORS
Ctra. de Marcà 5 - 43730 Falset
Tel.(977) 83 05 77
Fax,(977) 83 05 77

2. VITICULTORS MAS D'EN GIL
Pje, Mas d'en Gil - 43738 Bellmunt
Tel.(977)83.01.92
Fax.(93) 817 0167

3. FUENTES HERNANDEZ Josep M
Montsant, 2 - 43738 Bellmunt
Tel.(977) 83 06 48

4. VITICULTORS DEL PRIORAT
Mas Subirat - 43738 Bellmunt
Tel. (977) 26 22 68

5. VALL-LLACH MÁS MARTINENT
Vilanova, I - 4373 9 Porrera
Tel./Fax,(977) 82 8187

6. JOAN SANGENIS JUNCOSA
Prat do la Riba, 1
43739 Porrera
Tel.(977) 82 80 45

7. BODEGAS JOAN BLANCH
Pl. Màrtirs, 3 - 43739 Porrera
M.Aguiló 49 - 08005 Barcelona
Tel.(93) 307 45 04
Fax. .(93) 307 62 19

8. CELLER SANGENIS-VAQUÉ
Pl. Catalunya, 3 - 43739 Porrera
Tel.(977) 82 82 38

9. UNIO AGRARIA COOPERATIVA
Aptat 109 - 43280 Reus
Tel.(977) 33 00 55/60/65
Fax. (977) 33 00 70
Telex 56815 UNCOT E

10. VINICOLA DEL PRIORAT.
Paró, 33 - 43737 Gratallops
Tel./Fax (977) 83 9167

11. ASS.VIT. COSTERS DEL SILFRANA
Cami Manyetes, s/n 43737 Gratallops
Tel.(977) 83 92 76
Fax.(977)83 93 71

12. ALVARO PALACIOS
Valls, 24 - 43737 Gratallops
Tel.(977) 83 9195
Fax.(977) 83 9197

13. CLOS MOGADOR.
Cami Manyetes, s/n - 43737 Gratallops
Tel.(977) 83 9171
Fax,(977) 83 94 26

14. CELLER CECILIO
Piró, 30 - 43737 Gratallops
Tel.(977) 83 9181

15. CELLERS VILELLA DE LA CARTOIXA
Ereta, 10 - 43375 La Vilella Alta
Tel.(977) 83 92 99

16. DE MULLER
Plaça, 4 - 43379 Scala Dei

Cami Pedra Estela, 34 - 43205 Reus
Tel,(977) 75 62 65 - 75 34 73
Fax.(977) 77 1129

17. CELLERS SCALA DEI
Rbla. Cartoixa, 2 - 43379 Scala Dei
Tel.(977) 82 70 27
Fax.(977) 82 70 44

18. MASIA DUCH
Finca El Tancat - 4379 Scala Dei
Aptat. 1096 - 43280 Reus
Tel.(977) 77 35 13
Fax,(977) 34 12 15

19. LA CONRERIA D'SCALA DEI
Mitja Galta, 34 - 43379 Scala Dei
Tel.(977)82 70 63

20. ROTLLAN TORRA
Balandra, 6 - 43737 Torroja
Tel.(977) 83 92 85
Prim, 238 A, 7'2'- 08020 Barcelona
Tel.(93)313 43 47
Fax.(93) 305 01 12

21. PASANAU GERMANS
La Basa s/n 43361 La Morera de Montsant
Tel.(977) 82 72 02

22. MAS IGNEUS
Plaça, Portal, s/n - 43376 Poboleda
Tel.(977) 82 70 04
Fax.(977) 82 70 36

PRIORATO

Priorato draws its name from the 12th century Carthusian priory, one of Catalonia's oldest. It is said that one night a shepherd saw a stairway to heaven on the mountain, shown in the photo on facing page, hence Scala Dei (stairway to God) which is also depicted on the logo of the DO - and the name of the tiny village. The priory was established in 1163 and deserted in 1835. The area has pre-historic origins and the Romans were active in the area growing grapes and mining for silver and gold; today, wine is the liquid gold of the region.

On the way to the southern Priorato mountain wine country town of Gratallops, although it seems more suitable for mountain goats, the winelover's first lesson will be in road-building, something the Romans obviously brought from their mountain provinces. You will take the route N420, which runs through the centre of Reus, to Riudecols where the road starts to defy natural geography, clinging desperately to the sides of steep slopes. The N420 wanders uphill as a narrow windy road to the first of the panoramic undulating views approaching the important road centre of Falset, located in the southwest corner of Priorato comarca. While Falset is in the political boundary of Priorato, it is the main town in its own sub-zone of the Tarragona DO. In a wine sense it is not part of the Priorato DO, however this should not deter a visit.

An alternative, and even more pleasant route, C232, takes the aficionado from Reus through Alforja to the northern Priorato town of Poboleda which will lead onto Gratallops and down the slopes for the circular return journey.

This is a land for wine heroes. Rainfall is scant, therefore trickle irrigation is wisely common,

soils are slate stone, and yields are extremely low. All this adds up to highly concentrated and alcoholic wines, the minimum permissible is 13.5% but most often exceeded to astonishing levels - and high prices per bottle. This is not a problem as the value-for-money from good producers is exceptional and while this is the main, there are some poorly made wines at ridiculous prices - buyer beware. At this time the highest quality producers are: Clos Mogador (René Barbier - no connection with the giant of the same name) Clos Erasmus, Clos Martinet, Alvaro Palacios - stunning new cellar, Costers del Siurana, Masia Duch. Names to look for in the near future are the Penedès giant Miguel Torres and the smaller firm of Viñedos Ithaca.

While Priorato's reputation was established by a group of local and Tarragona enthusiasts, many smart "outsiders" are finding their way to these tricky slopes which vary from 200 - 1,000 metres above sea level. There is very little flat land and terraces which vary from one to four vine rows wide are used for plantings. Very little can be worked by machines of any description and mules are a common sight.

Grape plantings which are mainly for red wine are about equally divided between the Spanish varieties Garnacha and Cariñena and the French Cabernet and Syrah grapes. These make long-lived and powerhouse wines that need years in the bottle or hours in the glass to open-up and show their true majesty. Garnacha is at its best here and proves its greatness in, arguably, some of the world's finest and most expensive wines.

While needing years in the bottle, without fear, these wines will bring tears to the eyes of the most dedicated claret lover.

TARRAGONA

ALBESA FIGUEROLA
D'Avall, 34
43886 Vilabella
Tel. 977/ 62.01.90
Fax 977/ 62.01.90

BODEGA COOPERATIVA
Conde de Rius, 2
43360 Cornudella
Tel. 977/ 82.10.31
Fax 977/ 82.10.31

BODEGAS JOAN BLANCH
Aguiló, 49
08005 Barcelona
Tel. 93 307.45.04
Fax 93 307.62.19

BODEGAS MITJAVILA
Sant Cristófor, 29
43765 La Secuita
Tel. 977/ 61.11.31
Fax 411.24.07

CELLER SORT DEL CASTELL
Pl. Estació, 3
43760 El Morell
Tel. 977/ 84.06.55
Fax 977/ 84.21.46

CELLERS SERRA
Joan XXIII, 1
43791 Ascó
Tel. 977/ 40.50.15
Fax 977/ 40.61 10

COOP. AGR. EL MASROIG
Major, 8
43736 El Masroig
Tel. 977/ 82.50.50
Fax 977/ 82.53.15

COOP. AGR. FALSET
Miquel Barceló 31
43730 Falset
Tel. 977/ 83.01.05
Fax 977/ 83.03.63

COOP. AGR. CAPÇANES
Pau Casals, 33
43776 Capçanes
Tel. 977/ 17.81.53
Fax 977/ 17.81.53

COOP. AGR. ELS GUIAMETS
Esglèsia, 1
43777 Els Guiamets
Tel. 977/ 41.31.11
Fax 977/ 41.30.14

COOP. AGR. LA FIGUERA
Carretera, s/n
43736 La Figuera
Tel. 977/ 82.52.28
Fax 977/ 41.30 14

COOP. AGR. MARÇÀ
Dalt, 74
43775 Marçà
Tel. 977/ 17.83.66
Fax 977/ 17.83.66

COOP. AGR. MONTBRIÓ DEL CAMP
Avda. Sant Jordi, 19-21
43340 Montbrió del Camp
Tel. 977/ 82.60.39

COOP. AGR. NULLES
Raval de Sant Joan, 7
43887 Nulles
Tel. 977/ 60.26.22
Fax 977/ 60.26.22

COOP. AGR. SERRA D'ALMOS
Major, 23
43746 Serra d'Almos
Tel. 977/ 41.81.25
Fax 977/ 41.83.99

COOP. AGR. VALLS
Pl. del Carme, 9
43800 Valls
Tel. 977/ 60.05.21
Fax 977/ 60.06.54

COOP. AGR. VILA-RODONA
Av. Enric Benet, 4
4314 Vila-rodona
Tel. 977/ 63.80.04
Fax 977/ 63.90.75

DALMAU HNOS. I CIA
Pol. Industrial Francolí, nau 11
4380 Tarragona
Tel. 977/ 54.21.00
Fax 977/ 54.12.27

DE MULLER
Cami Pedra Estela, 34
43205 Reus
Tel. 977/ 75.74.73
Fax 977/ 77.11.29

EMILIO MIRÓ SALVAT
Adrià Gual, 10
43280 Reus
Tel. 977/ 31.29.58
Fax 977/ 32,03.21

FRANSESC MASDEU PERPIÑÀ
Major, 99
43736 El Masroig
Tel. 977/ 82.50.17

FRANCISCO CAPAFONS BES
Vallmoreres, 4
43730 Falset
Tel. 977/ 77.17.93
Fax 977/ 75.79.45

JOSEP ANGUERA BEYME
Major, 29
43746 Darmos-Tivissa
Tel. 977/ 41.83.02
Fax 977/ 41.83.02

JOSEP M SAUMELL CALAF
Sant Antoni, 5
43812 Rodonyà
Tel. 977/ 62.83.05
Fax 977/ 62.83.05

LA VINÍCOLA MESTRE
Apartat de Correus, 101
43080 Tarragona
Tel. 977/ 62.52.26
Fax 977/ 62.53.78

MARC VIDAL MAS
Compte Arnau, 5
43330 Riudoms
Tel. 977/ 85.04.10

TOUS ANDREU
Unió, 9
43001 Tarragona
Tel. 977/ 23.67.16
Fax 977/ 23.86.31

UNIÓ AGÀRIA COOP
Apartat Correus, 109
43280 Reus
Tel. 977/ 33.00.55
Fax 977/ 33.00.70

VINÍCOLA DE LA RIBERA
Av. Mn. Cinto Verdaguer, 3
43770 Mora la Nova
Tel. 977/ 40.03.50
Fax 977/ 40.30.76

VINS PADRÓ
Avgda. Catalunya, 56-58
43812 Brafim
Tel. 977/ 62.00.12
Fax 977/ 62.04.86

TARRAGONA

A 2000-year-old Roman amphitheatre overlooking the Mediterranean is an impressive site and a splendid introduction to a major port city just oozing with history. There is also deeply-rooted culture among Tarragona's many other fascinating attractions such as seafood and education. After Barcelona, Tarragona port is Catalonia's second in size but far senior in age and history. In addition to being the early port for Carthaginians and Greeks at the western end of the Mediterranean, it was also the capital on Roman Spain bearing the name of Tarraco.

At least a century prior to the birth of Jesus Christ, Tarraconese wines were being shipped to Rome and, 2100 years later, sacramental wines are still being sent to the Vatican - and many other countries around the world.

To explore the wonders of the Tarragona province, one of Catalonia's four provinces, the winelover should consider staying in the attractive city of Reus (ray-oos), just 12 kilometres from Tarragona, and former home of the legendary cellist Pau Casals. We found the Hotel NH Ciudad de Reus a wonderful base. Reus, with a population of 100,000 folks, is a strategic commercial centre with its share of industry but it is also the shopfront for many neighbouring towns. It is said that all roads lead to Rome, this is also true of Reus. It is easy to become shopped-out in one day; Reus is a town for the rugged three day shopper.

Here in this thriving suburbia, with grapevines growing right up to the very edge of the city, history has been very carefully preserved and the city's new structures blend harmoniously with the old. To avoid visual pollution, all city car parks are located underground.

Tarragona boasts one of Catalonia's largest DOs that, due to its unwieldy size and laziness of its Consejo Regulador, is divided into three sub-zones: Tarragona Campo (region) on the alluvial soils of the Ebro River delta, Ribera Ebro and Falset. As a supplier of fine wines Tarragona has become a backwater since the move of top producer De Muller from the waterfront to Reus. With its incredible aged dessert wines and sacramental wines which have been shipped to churches the world over, De Muller was the icon of Tarragona.

Although the company has moved only 15 kilometres and is still within the DO, the company under new ownership, has a new face and profile. Major plantings of 128 ha surround the Reus bodega, the company also has further vineyards in Terra Alta and Priorato. The company recommends *Priorat de Muller* as its top wine. A blend of 60% Garnacha, 30% Cabernet and 30% Cariñena with an alcohol level of 13.5% and 5.1 acidity, this wine shows all the hallmarks of what cannot be achieved with Tarragona grapes. One of De Muller's 80 year old, 55,000 litre vats is pictured opposite.

Unfortunately, Tarragona is dominated by co-operatives producing wines mainly suitable for supermarket specials; of the 30 DO wineries 12 are cooperatives. The Falset cooperative, with a mass of new equipment and, above all, new thinking, and an increased elevation from the coastal plains, has broken from the traditional co-op role and watches closely what is happening in Priorato in both quality and price.

Josep A Beyme, in Darmos-Tivissa, is a worthy producer showing what is possible in Tarragona.

COSTERS DEL SEGRE

Costers del Segre is a contradiction in every way. The DO is certainly classic Mediterranean, but not the climate. Being more than 100 km inland, it has a far more Continental climate than those regions closer to the coast - hotter summers and cooler winters, even snow. This dictates which grapes will do best in a particular region and right from the very start it was evident that the local varieties from the coastal areas were not going to make great wines.

Although grapes have been grown in the region for eons, it was the work of a visionary, Manuel Raventós, who established the region, and his property Raimat, as one of Spain's best. However, this was done not with Spanish thinking, rather with a totally American bias and advice. The California university consultants recommended traditional French grape varieties to a man who had pioneered the use of Spanish grape varieties for cava. He adopted California viticultural practices and American oak barrels despite being only a few hundred kilometres from French oak forests.

To survive, this land with an annual rainfall of 300 mm needs irrigation, generally something that is foolishly disallowed in most Spanish vineyards. Humans are not allowed in the scorching sun without liquids for even one day, but a grape vine is expected to survive a whole summer in desert conditions without a drink! Does this make sense? Changes are pending.

Raventós, owning one third of all grapes and most of the best wine produced in Costers del Segre, was responsible for this relatively small area of grapes (3,700 ha) becoming a DO. Centred on the city of Lérida, the DO has the Raimat sub-zone only 15 km to the west and three sub-zones east of Lérida. Valls de Ríu Corb and Les Garrigues are neighbours, while Artesa stands alone in the north. With few exceptions, wines produced in these regions are very ordinary and either go for cava or local sales.

However, there are exceptions to every rule and at least one good producer can be found in each region. Raimat is a class act with stunning wines that can be purchased worldwide. The two Cabernets - Mas Castell and Vallcorba are among Spain's finest red wines and at half the price of the top Priorato wines, they represent excellent value. Today, Raimat produces around 210,000 cases annually.

In the north, Vall de Baldomar stars, in the Valls de Ríu Corb, L'Olivera Co-op and Castell de Remei will not disappoint with either white, rosé or red wine.

AGROPEQUARIA l'OLIVERA
La Plana, s/n
25268 Vallbona de les Monges
Tel. 973/ 33.02.76
Fax 973/ 33.02.76

CAMERLOT
Crta. lvars-Castellserà
25333 Castell del Remei
Tel. 973/ 57.00.89
Fax 973/ 57.05.11

CARVIRESA
Avgda. Tarragona, s/n
25300 Tàrrega
Tel. 973/ 31.07.32
Fax 973/ 31.06.16

CELLER DE CANTONELLA
Av. Garrigues, 26
25471 La Pobla de CŠrvoles
Tel. 973/ 17.51.01
Fax 973/ 57.05.11

CODORNIU - RAIMAT
Gran Via, 644
08007 Barcelona
Tel. 93 301.46.00
Fax 93 301.39.47

VERDUVIN
Carretera, 19
25340 Verdú
Tel. 973/ 34.70.65
Fax 973/ 34.70.65

JAUME BONET MINGUELLA
Camí Tàrrega s/n
25752 L'Ametlla Age la Segarra

JOSEP TORRES CUCURULL
Bonaire, 19
25340 Verdú
Tel. 973 34.70.23

MONESTIR DEL TALLAT
Finca Falla
43449 Els Omellos de Na Gaia
Tel. 977 84.06.55
Fax 977 84.24.16

SAT VALL DE BALDOMAR
La Font, s/n
25737 Baldomar

Conca de Barbera

Rather than speeding along the autopista from Reus or Tarragona back to Vilafranca, another pleasant trip can be had by taking a route through the well sign-posted Montblanc. This is the capital of Conca de Barbera DO which draws its name from the historic, small village of Barbera de Conca (500 people) at the confluence of the Francolí and Anguera Rivers. Conca means a basin or hollow. Conca de Barbera is known for its hazelnuts and almonds although the area is linked to Penedès by cereal fields and the WELCOME TO PENEDÈS DO sign is firmly embedded in a field of oats rather than grapes.

Due west of Penedès and averaging about 500 metres above seal level, Conca de Barbera is similar to, and a continuation of, the high Penedès region where Chardonnay and Pinot noir show their greatest expression in Spain. In selected areas, Cabernet Sauvignon equals this top quality and is best portrayed in Torres Gran Coronas.

The monastery of Poblet, established by the Cistercians in 1151, was the most powerful religious house in Catalonia for many centuries, and is today a magnet for tourists. During their heyday, the Cistercians built other fortresses such as Milmanda, Riudabella and Castefollit. While all three are well-known to local tourists, Milmanda is the top name on the international wine circuit as the source of Torres Milmanda Chardonnay; one of the world's finest.

Much of Conca de Barbera grape production, unfortunately or otherwise, disappears into Penedès cava houses thus robbing the DO of any recognition. With its admirable terroir for growing outstanding flavoured grapes, it is surprising that a lot more world-class wineries have not been established in the region.

The principal winery, Concavins, formerly a bankrupted co-operative, is now a stellar operation incorporating excellent grapes resources, the latest technology in the winery, and international consultants.

Conca de Barbera DO has 14 wine communities and 15 wineries. Six of these are co-operatives; there are but nine private bodegas It is for this reason that there has been an ongoing under-current of activity to embrace Conca de Barbera within the much larger Penedès DO, a sound idea that is too practical to happen.

The DO capital Montblanc is a national monument, definitely worth a visit, as is Espluga de Francolí, a nice town containing several national monuments.

ANTONI SANS ESPAÑOL
Gral. Mola,10,
43412 Solivella
Tel. 977/89.21.65
Fax 977/89.20.73

CARIES ANDREU DOMINGO
Doctor Robert, 8
43424 Pira
Tel. 977/88.70.05

CONCAVINS & H. RYMAN
Crta. Montblanc-Barber
Km. 9.800
43422 Barberà de la Conca
Tel. 977/88.70.30
Fax 977/88.70.32

EMILI MATEU MATEU
14 de gener, 44
43424 Sarral
Tel. 977/89.00.32
Fax 977/89.04.71

LA XARMADA
Miquel Alfonso, 1
43400 Montblanc
Tel. 977/86,23.88
Fax 977/817.15.46

RENDÉ MASDEU
Av. Catalunya, 44
43440 L'espluga de Francolí
Tel. 977/87.13.67

RIUDABELLA
Apartat de correus 29
43440 L'espluga de Francolí
Tel. 977/87.80.40

ROSA MA. TORRES
Av. Anguera, 2
43424 Sarral
Tel. 977/89.01.73
Fax 977/89.01.73

SIMÓ DE PALAU
Crta.N-240 Km. 39
43440 L'Espluga de Francollí
Tel. 977/86.25.99
Fax 977/87.10.53

AMPURDÁN - COSTA BRAVA

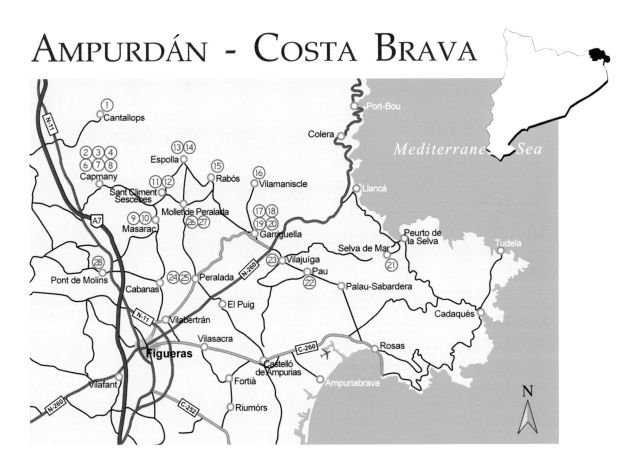

1. **MASIA SERRA**
c/ Dels Solés, 20 Tel: 9726 73407
17708 CANTALLOPS

2. **OLIVEDA**
c/ La Roca, 3 Tel: 9725 49012
17750 CAPMANY

3. **PERE GUARDIOLA**
c/ Centre, 3 Tel. 9725 49024
17750 CAPMANY

4. **CELLERS SANTAMARIA**
Placa, 6 Tel: 9725 49022
17750 CAPMANY

6. **PAGÉS VIÑAS**, Mariano
C/ PuJada, 6 Tel: 9725 49160
17750 CAPMANY

7. **COOP AGRÍ EL PARRAL**
c/ Sant Climent, s/n Tel. 9725 49094
17750 CAPMANY

8. **CELLER OLIVER CONTI**
c/ Puignau, s/n Tel: 9721 93161
1775O CAPMANY

9. **ALBERT FITA ALEGRE**
Celler Mas Fita Tel: 9725 02041
17763 MASARAC

10. **COOP AGRÍ MASARACH**
Barri Priorat, s/n Tel:
17763 MASARAC

11. **COOP AGRÍ SANT CLIMENT SESCEBES**
c/Del Sol, s/n. Tel: 9725 63370
17751 SANT CLIMENT SESCEBES

12. **MARTÍ FABRA CARRERAS**
Barri de Vic, 26 T
Tel: 9725 63011
17751 SANT CLIMENT SESCEBES

13. **AGUSTINA TUGERT MOLAS**
c/ Carme, 1 Tel. 9725 63061
17753 ESPOLLA

14. **CELLER COOP D'ESPOLLA**
Tel, 9725 63049
17753 ESPOLLA

15. **COOP AGRÍ SANT JULIÁ**
Ctra. de Roses, s/n - Tel. 9725 63426
17754 RABÓS D'EMPORDA

16. **COOP AGRÍ VILAMANISCLE**
c/ Lluis Pagès 7
17781 VILAMNISCLE

17. **BODEGAS TROBAT**
c/ Castelló, 5 Tel. 9725 30092
17780 GARRIGUELLA

18. **XAVIER MASET ISACH**
Placa de L'Egléssia, 3 Tel: 9725 30096
 17750 GARRIGUELLA

19. **MAIRE DE DÉU DEL CAMP**
c/ Sant Ferran, 7 Tel. 9725 30085
17780 GARRIGUELLA

20. **COOP AGRÍCOLA GARRIGUELLA**
Ctra. de Roses, s/n Tel. 9725 30002
17780 GARRIGUELILA

21. **SODA**
Mas Estela, Tel: 9721 26176
17469 SELVA DE MAR

22. **COOPERATIVA AGRÍ DE PAU**
Ctra. de Roses, s/n Tel 9725 30140
17494 PAU

23. **COOP. VITIVÍNCOLA ALT EMPORDA**
Ctra. de Roses, 3 Tel.9725 30043
17493 VILAJUÍGA

24. **CAVAS DEL CASTILLO DE PERELADA**
Placa del Carme, I - Tel. 9725 3801
17491 PERALADA

25. **CAVAS DEL AMPURDÁN**
Paratge La Granja Tel:
17491 PERALADA

26. **COOP AGRÍ MOLLET DE PERALADA**
c/ Espolla, 9 Tel: 9725 63150
17752 MOLLET DE PERALADA

27. **COVINOSA**
c/ Espolla, 9 - Tel. ~ 9725 63150
17752 MOLLET DE PERALADA

28. **COOP AGRÍ RICARDELL**
Ctra. de Madrid a Franca s/n - Tel.
9725 29219
17706 PONT DE MOLINS

AMPURDÀN - COSTA BRAVA

Once you are on the autopista A7 or the N11, from Barcelona or Vilafranca, heading towards the obligatory stop at Figueres and the Dalí museum, you will quickly realize that you are in a different place. For 100 kilometres there are no visible grape vines. What you see instead are vegetable and flower hothouses clinging to the sides of hills or managed forests of trees to supply matches for the endless number of Spanish chain-smokers. The countryside becomes greener as you travel north and realize that rainfall at about 800 millimetres annually is much higher than in Penedès.

Bounded by the dazzling Pyrenees mountains and France in the north, and the Mediterranean on the eastern side, Ampurdán-Costa Brava with its double-barreled name, is one of many attractions. Horror of all horrors, should the visitor tire of Catalan food then it is a simple 20 kilometre drive to the land of frogs legs and snails.

This close proximity to France has had considerable impact on the wine styles of the past and present. While Garnacha and Cariñena have been the heart of red wine production, despite the fact that rosé is the preferred wine style, most new plantings are of the French varieties Cabernet Sauvignon, Syrah, Merlot for red wine and, sensibly, Chardonnay and Chenin for white wine. As this is very much cava country, the three local Catalan white grapes are in most vineyards. Tempranillo is also meeting with considerable success.

As mentioned on page 23, although soils and the Mediterranean climate are amenable, the winds of this Ampurdán-Costa Brava region are notorious for reaching speeds of up to 150 kilometres per hour! This hazard requires careful management in the vineyards and even more careful selection of vineyard sites. Most of the wines produced come from the relatively low plains country which sweep to the sea, and the 10 cooperatives which dominate production in the region.

The small village of Capmany, with six bodegas, is a strong production centre together with two excellent and friendly producers - Oliveda and Pere Guardiloa. Oliveda is quite outstanding in the whole of Catalonia with an excellent showroom full of gifts and knowledgeable staff. They will tempt you with everything from Chardonnay to sweet Garnacha liqueur wines, including a superb Rigau-Ros Gran Reserva red wine comprising 50 percent Garnacha and Cabernet Sauvignon. This firm makes intelligent blends across the spectrum of joven, crianza and reserva wines - both red and white.

Another important town for the wine and history aficionado is the more swinging Peralada. It is home to a casino, an historic castle and the bodega, another excellent large producer, Castillo del Perelada which produces around 600,000 cases annually. This is a big and good operation with an adjoining public restaurant and a casino just across the road.

For the truly adventurous winelover, a visit to the Mas Estela vineyard and winery at La Selva de Mar is an absolute must. Mind you, Mas Estela is possibly Spain's most difficult to find location, but, being the only bodega for some distance, all the locals can direct you. It is farmed by the parents and three sons who produce not only superb wine, but also their own electricity and water. This is a class act and the Syrah is something else. There are also wonderful red Garnacha, Chardonnay and Moscatel wines.

To write about the history of this symbolic region would take a book on its own but suffice to say that this is the original home of wine in Catalonia; a place where the first ever book on the subject of wine and viticulture in Spain was written. This treasured book is now firmly ensconced in a Paris museum. As a tourist destination the Costa Brava attracts literally millions of people from around the globe - yet we found that there was still room for many more - without any problems.

PLA DE BAGES

DENOMINACIÓ D'ORIGEN
Pla de Bages

The wine regions north of Penedès are best visited from the great city of Barcelona. Two major roads lead from the city to the interesting wine region of Pla del Bages (supposedly named after Bacchus) - a highway via Martorell and there is also the autopista via Terrassa, both heading in the direction of Manresa - and Paris!

Manresa, about 65 km north west of Barcelona, is almost the centre of Catalonia and the region is known as the central depression. Everywhere among the 18 wine communities making-up the DO, there is history, crumbled castles and high peaks. The region has many similarities to the high Penedès including ample rainfall exceeding 500 mm annually.

From the Manresa area one can obtain another view of the Catalan icon, Montserrat - from the north rather than from the south. The shortest route to the mountain and monastic scenic attractions is from the city of Manresa, located on the River Llobregat.

Originally the region was called Artès after one of the principal growing areas, Pla de Bages became a DO as recently as 1996.

The main wine growing towns are on a south-west - northeast axis about 20 km in each direction from Manresa. Historically the favoured grape varieties have been the native Catalan varieties Macabeo and Picapoll, another less well-know variety for making everyday white wines. Much of the Macabeo production finds its way to the cava houses of Penedès.

Tempranillo and Garnacha have been the mainstays for rosada and red wines but, to the credit of the region, these local varieties are now being blended with Cabernet Sauvignon and Merlot. Like most other regions, Pla del Bages has also been caught up in the international craze for Chardonnay which is now a popular style, and at times, Chardonnay is blended with Picapoll, a little known Catalan variety.

If the visitor has time only for one visit, Masies D'Avinyó is suggested.

CELLER COOP. ARTÉS
Rocafort, 36
08271 Artes
Tel. 93 830.53.25
Fax 93 830.53.25

CELLER COOP. SALELLES
Crta. Igualda, s/n
08240 Manresa
Tel. 93 872.05.72
Fax 93 872.05.72

JOAQUIM FARGAS FÀRGAS
Casa Quico
08253 Sant Salvador Guardiola
Tel. 93 835.85.47

JOSEP SOLER GIBERT SERRA
Barquera, 40
08271 Artes
Tel. 93 830,50.84
Fax 93 830,50.84

MAS DE SANT ISCLE
Barri de Sant Iscle
08272 Sant Fruites de Bages
Tel. 93 874.69.59

MASIES D'AVINYÓ
Crta. Vic, 83
08240 Manresa
Tel. 93 874.35.11
Fax 93 873.72.04

VINS GRAU
Ctra. Igualada-Manresa, km. 11
08259 Maians (Castellfollit del Boix)
Tel. 93 835.60.02

ALELLA

No sooner do you leave the north eastern boundary of Barcelona on the autopista A19 heading for Mataro, than you come to the exits for Tiana, then Alella, two towns of the Alella DO. Alella is a mere 14 km from the vibrant Barcelona city centre. With only three operating wineries, this is one of the smallest appellations (570 hectares of grapes) in Spain. Still, should you be a visitor or a resident of Barcelona, it is not an area that can be ignored.

Even though the region is being choked by urban sprawl, in recent years the Consejo Regulador has expanded the limits where grapes can be grown to qualify for the DO label. This new area in the higher lands has, in part, compensated for the developers' thrust along the coastal strip.

Ruefully, this region of 400 hectares of vines has adopted the Catalan name of Pansa Blanc for its important white variety Xarel-lo, and Ull de Lebre for Tempranillo. This nonsense does nothing but confuse the already confused wine buyer and the Consejo Regulador could set an example by sticking with the accepted norms, even if Tempranillo is widely known by the Catalan name Ull de Lebre - in Catalonia only.

The three wineries operating in Alella are all doing good to excellent work. Two are in new premises and there is a strong desire locally for innovation and well packaged products.

The Alella cooperative, situated right in the centre of Alella, is unusual in that it bottles every drop of wine under its well-respected Marfil label. Another Alella producer, Bodegas Roura, has built a new facility in the Rials Valley to keep up with the times. Roura runs counter to other producers by making a full range of cava and white wines - rosé and red wines from Cabernet, Merlot and Tempranillo. Under the Roura label, the Merlot rosé is a runaway favourite. Chardonnays are bottled under both the Roura and Voromar labels

Marqués de Alella which is the Parxet label for its still wines, bases its production totally on white wine using Macabeo, Parellada and Xarel-lo for much of their wine. These are supported by Chardonnay and Chenin.

ALLELLA VINÍCOLA
Rambla Angel Guimerà, 62
08328 Alella
Tel. 93 540,38.42
Fax 93 540.16.48

BODEGAS ROURA
Valle de Rials, s/n
08328 Alella
Tel. 93 352.74.56
Fax 93 352.43.39

PARXET
Torrent, 38
08391 Tiana
Tel. 93 395.08.11
Fax 93 395.55.00

TERRA ALTA

The literal translation of Terra Alta is high land - and at an average height of about 400 metres that is half of the story. The other half is that this plateaud basin is surrounded by peaks ranging in height from 700 - 1,000 metres. Such an individual landscape makes for a Continental climate similar to Costers del Segre - hot summers and freezing winters. In addition to being the most southern DO, this landscape also makes for isolation and, really, Terra Alta did not come into the scheme of Catalan wine until the 20th century.

Gaudí architect student, Cèsar Martinell, was a very busy person designing and building many churches and wine cooperatives in southern Catalonia and samples of his classics can be seen in the cooperatives at Falset and the Modernist structure at Gandesa, wine capital of Terra Alta.

The annual rainfall of only 400 mm supports 10,000 ha of vines in 12 municipalities. The white Garnacha, eventually supported by Macabeo

have been the mainstay of white wine production, with a goodly percentage going-off to the Penedès cava houses. Traditionally, red Garnacha and Carineña were the king of the red wines but this has changed in recent years and one can now readily find wines made from Cabernet and Merlot. However, not a lot of wine is bottled, much is sold in bulk - but with an influx of new thinkers such as the Gandesa Co-op, Pedro Rovira and the re-invigorated Bàrbara Forés label, it is possible that a new millennium will bring better results.

Reus is a good base to visit this region. The N420 provides a steady run to Gandesa through Falset. There is much history here including one of the Civil War's bloodiest battles costing over 60,000 lives -a tragedy too sad to believe.

The Knights Templars, early settlers in the region, would be pleased at the re-organization and modernization of this fledgling industry.

BODEGAS CORTIELLA
Avgda. Terra Alta, 47
43784 Corbera d'Ebre
Tel. 977/ 42.04.34
Fax 977/ 42.04.34

CELLERS MARIOL
Les Forques, s/n
43786 Batea
Tel. 977/ 43.03.03
Fax 977/ 43.03.03

CELLERS TARRONE
Calvari, 22
43786 Batea
Tel. 977/ 43.01.09
Fax 977/ 43.01.83

CELLERS VIDAL I VIDAL
Plaça de la Vila, 2
43782 Vilalba dels Arcs
Tel. 977/ 43.81.52

COMERCIAL BORRAS VALLESPÍ
Acres, 21
43782 Vilalba dels Arcs
Tel. 977/ 43.80.36

DEMULLER
Cami Pedra Estela, 34
43205 Reus
Tel. 977/ 75.74.73
Fax 977/ 77.11.29

FERRER ESCODA
Santa Anna, 28
43780 Gandesa
Tel. 977/ 42,01.60
Fax 977142,01,60

FRANCISCO DE RIBAS DE SALAS
Vergós 22
08017 Barcelona
Tel. 93 203 92.50

JOSÉ VALLS
Mendez Núñez s/n
43780 Gandesa
Tel. 977/ 42.02.93

JUAN VICENTE CLUA JULVE
Onze de Setembre, 8
43597 Arnes
Tel. 977/ 43.51.39

LA BOTERA
Sant Roc, 26
43786 Batea
Tel. 977/ 43.00.09

PEDRO ROVIRA
Mn. Cinto Verdaguer, 3
43770 Mora la Nova
Tel. 977/ 40.03.59

VINS PIÑOL
Av. Aragó 9
43786 Batea
Tel. 977/ 43.05.05
Fax 977143.05.05

XAVIER CLUA COMA
Angel, 18
43782 Vilalba dels Arcs
Tel. 977/ 43.80.13

CATALAN  CUISINE

Red Meat

Desserts   Eggs

Poultry   Fish

Cheese   Yoghurt

Olive Oil   Wine

Fruit   Dried Fruit   Nuts &   Vegetables
Legumes

Bread Pasta Rice Cereals Potatoes

BORGES

Garlic Sauce

Picada

The Sauces (Salses)

Garlic Sauce (Allioli)

Used since Roman times, this classic, all purpose Catalan sauce corresponds to the aioli of Provence and is served with grills, roast meat, fish and vegetables. Purists insist that it be made without eggs, but many alliolis (in common with aioli) do contain eggs - which makes them considerably easier to prepare, but more like mayonnaise.

Makes approximately 150 ml   2/3 cup
Ingredients: **6 cloves garlic - salt - 30 ml/2 tbsp parsley, chopped - 150 ml 2/3 cup virgin olive oil - a little lemon juice**

Method Crush the garlic in a mortar with a little salt and the parsley. Drip in the olive oil little by little, stirring all the while with a wooden spoon, add the lemon juice and continue stirring until the sauce thickens like a mayonnaise. This may also be done in a blender or food processor.
A variety of other ingredients are sometimes incorporated in the basic recipe, often an egg yolk.

Picada

For a recipe serving 4—6

This is one of the five basic Catalan sauces. it is made from almonds or the hazelnuts so extensively grown in Catalonia, saffron, fried bread and other ingredients. It has been likened to roux, in that it is often stirred into a dish towards the end of cooking to thicken it and enhance the flavour.

Ingredients: **4 fingers white bread virgin olive oil - 50 g/½ cup roasted almonds and/or hazelnuts, skinned - few strands of saffron - 2 large cloves garlic, peeled**

Method: First fry the fingers of bread in hot olive oil, then pound all the ingredients in in a mortar to a smooth paste. Dilute with a spoonful of the liquid from the dish for which it is intended (whether fish, shellfish or game) and stir together well. Picada is usually added during the last stages of cooking.

Bread With Tomato

Savoury Fish Pate

The Starters

Bread With Tomato
(Pa amb tomaquet)

This is a Catalan favourite, eaten at home for breakfast or before other meals and often served in small restaurants. It consists of country bread, either fresh or toasted, rubbed with fresh garlic and tomato and sprinkled with olive oil and salt. It is sometimes accompanied with cured ham or anchovies.

Savoury Fish Pate
(Garum)

Most famous and costly of the sauces used in Roman cookery, garum was largely supplied to Rome by establishments along the Mediterranean coast around Cartagena. It was made in large vessels by layering assorted cut-up fish with herbs, with salt as a preservative. Though hardly the same thing, a modified garum is made by the master chef Jaume Subirós at the Hotel-Restaurant Ampurdán in Figueres, to whom we are indebted for this recipe.

Ingredients: **2 tins (100 g) of anchovies, soaked in milk for 1 hour and patted dry - 2 x 15 ml spoons/2 tbsp capers, drained - I large clove of garlic, chopped - 25 ml/2 tbsp brandy - 400 g/2½ cups stoned black olives - 5 ml/1 tsp fresh thyme, ground - 5 ml/1 tsp rosemary, ground - 5 ml/1 tsp flat-leaved parsley, ground - 2 hard-boiled eggs, -yolks separated and whites chopped very fine - 150 ml/2/3 cup virgin olive oil - freshly ground pepper**

Method Make a smooth paste in a food processor of all the ingredients less the oil, pepper and whites of egg, then reduce the speed and drop in the oil as if making mayonnaise. Season with pepper and transfer to a bowl, cool and decorate with the chopped white of egg. Serve with toast.

Catalan Style Spinach

Chicken with Prawns

Catalan Style Spinach
(Espinacs a la Catalana)

Serves 4

This dish is often served as a starter in country restaurants and makes use of the pine kernels so often used in Catalan cookery.

Ingredients

2 x tbsp olive oil - 2 x cloves garlic, finely chopped - 2 anchovies, soaked in milk for 1/2 hour - and cut up - I kg spinach or Swiss chard, boiled in salted water and well-drained - 50 g/1/3 cup pine kernels - 50 g/¼ cup raisins
salt and freshly ground pepper

Method: Heat the oil in a pan and fry the garlic briefly, taking care not to blacken it. Add the anchovies and spinach, stir gently while adding the pine kernels and raisins. Season with salt and pepper and cook on a low heat for about 10 minutes until very tender.

Chicken with Prawns
(Pollastre amb gambes)

Ingredients: **4 x 15 ml spoons/4 tbsp olive oil - flour for dusting'**
2 chicken breasts, cut into 4 pieces and dredged in flour - 1 small onion, finely chopped
2 cloves garlic, finely chopped - 150 ml/2/3 cup Catalan brandy - 15 ml spoon/1 tbsp corn flour - 300 ml/10 fl oz/11/3 cup chicken stock - salt and pepper - 30 ml/2 tbsp flat parsley, finely chopped - 450 g/I lb fresh prawns, boiled and peeled

Method: Heat the olive oil in a large casserole, brown the breasts of chicken, remove and reserve. In the same pan fry the onion until soft, then add the garlic, stirring well, and cook for one minute. Pour in the brandy and flame, stirring until the flames subside. Stir in the corn flour add the chicken stock and season to taste with freshly ground salt and pepper. Now add half of the parsley and the chicken pieces and cook very slowly for about 20 minutes until the chicken is very tender, adding the prawns 5 minutes before the chicken is ready, and stirring gently together. Garnish with the remaining parsley and serve.

Catalan Fish and Potato Soup

Catalan Fish and Potato Soup
(Suquet)

This is one of the best-known and most delicious of scores of Catalan fish soups and stews. Like the romesco de peix which gave its name to the famous romesco sauce, it was first made by the fishermen at sea by dressing up the less saleable of their catch.

Fish fumée

(Ingredients)

1 litre/35 fl oz/4½ cups water, trimmings from the fish (heads and bones)

450 g/1 lb/I lb rascasse (if available), cut up

1 leek

1 carrot

1 onion

5 sprigs parsley with stalks

1 bay leaf 2 sprigs mint

juice of ½ lemon

4 potatoes, peeled and cut up

1 kg/2 lb/2 lb fish and shellfish, e.g. prawns and a selection of halibut, sea bass, monkfish or other firm white fish cut into steaks

flour for dusting

salt and pepper

olive oil

300 ml/ 10 fl oz/ 1½ cup fish fumée

2 cloves garlic, finely chopped

15 ml spoon/I tbsp/1 tbsp flat-leaved parsley

25 ml/1 fl oz/2 tbsp brandy

sofregit

picada - with added bread - 4 rounds instead of 4 fingers

Method:

To make the fumée, wash the fish trimmings and rascasse. Simmer gently with all ingredients except potatoes, removing the scum, for about 30-40 minutes until the liquid is reduced to half. Strain, boil the potatoes in it for 15 minutes.

Fry the shellfish briefly in a little olive oil, peel and reserve. Dust the white fish in seasoned flour, Fry the fish, a few pieces at a time, in hot olive oil until golden. Put on a plate and when cool enough remove bones and skin and break into smaller pieces. Return shellfish and fish to the frying pan , add garlic, parsley and brandy and flambé. Now add the *sofriget* and the *picada* with the extra fried bread, and transfer to the pan with the fumèe and potatoes. Check the seasoning, stir well and heat together until very hot for 5 - 8 minutes for the flavours to mingle.

Shellfish Stew Catalan Style

Shellfish Stew Catalan Style
(Sarsuela de marisca la catalana)

Sarsuela (perhaps more familiar in the Castilian spelling 'zarzuela') means a variety show, and you may ring the changes on this magnificent fish stew, provided that any white fish used is firm and does not disintegrate in cooking.
Serves 6

Ingredients
12 clams or 24 mussels, well scrubbed and washed in cold water
100 ml1/4 fl oz/½ cup olive oil
1 onion, chopped
250 g/9 oz/9 oz squid, cleaned and cut into rings
250 g/9 oz/9 oz sea bass or hake, sliced
250 g/9 oz/9 oz angler fish, sliced
250 g/9 oz/9 oz prawns in shell, boiled
8 scampi in shell, boiled
30 ml/2 tbsp/2 tbsp Spanish brandy
I clove garlic, crushed
15 mI/1 tbsp/1 tbsp tomato purèe
50 ml/2 fl oz/¼cup dry white wine
salt and pepper
15 ml spoon/1 tbsp/1 tbsp chopped parsley
4 fingers fried white bread, without crusts
few strands saffron
12 roasted almonds, skinned

Method
Bring the clams to boil in water, leave them until they open, then drain and reserve them with the stock.
Heat the olive oil in a large, deep casserole, fry the onion for 10 minutes, then add the squid, sea bass or hake, angler fish, the prawns and scampi, and fry together until brown. Pour in the brandy and flambé. Add the garlic, tomato purèe, wine and reserved stock. Season with salt, pepper and parsley, stir together well and cook slowly for 20 minutes, uncovered, adding a little hot water if necessary. Ten minutes before removing from the heat, add the clams. Grind the fresh bread, saffron and almonds to a paste, dissolve with a little of the stock, and stir this picada into the stew. Serve immediately

Baked Custard with Brittle Caramel

Desserts
(Postres)

Baked Custard with Brittle Caramel
(Crema catalana)

A version of the flan de huevos popular all over Spain, this is perhaps the best-known of Catalan desserts.
Serves 6

Ingredients:
6 egg yolks, beaten
25 g/1 oz/3 tbsp cornflour
175 g/6 oz/1½ cups icing sugar
500 ml/17 fl oz/2½ cups milk
1 cinnamon stick
rind of 1 lemon
2 x 15 ml spoons/2 tbsp/2 tbsp brown sugar

Method:
Put the egg yolks in a bowl with the cornflour and icing sugar. Simmer the milk with the cinnamon stick and lemon rind, then add the egg mixture and cook slowly to avoid lumps until the custard thickens - do not boil it. This may be done in a large double boiler or in a saucepan placed in a larger pan of boiling water. Remove the cinnamon stick and lemon rind, divide the custard between 6 x 7.5 cm (3 inch) ramekins, and leave to cool in the refrigerator overnight.
Before serving, sprinkle the top with brown sugar and leave for a few seconds under a hot grill, then cool again. Do this about 30 minutes beforehand so that the caramel remains crisp.

GLOSSARY

Acetic bacteria: Turns alcohol into water and acetic acid. Vinegar is a form of acetic acid.

Acidity: Tartness; the sharp taste of natural grape acid. Contributes to the flavour and keeping qualities. Not to be confused with sourness.

Acescence: Referring to sour taste, possibly from acetic acid.

After-flavour: The wine flavour remaining in the mouth.

Ampelography: Study of grapes.

Aroma: The smell of the wine from the grape, as opposed to bouquet coming from winemaking contributions.

Aromatic: Fragrant, a richness of aroma and flavour, from aromatic grape varieties like Muscat, Riesling, Traminer.

Astringent: A dry, mouth-puckering effect caused by a high tannin content. May soften as the wine matures.

Austere: A tough and severe wine; simple, lacking in complexity.

Baked: Hot and cooked smell produced by burnt and shrivelled grapes due to excessive sunshine.

Balance: The combination and relationship of component parts.

Baumé: Used in Australia and Portugal as a measure of sugar in grape juice or wine. One degree of baume equals 1.8 percentage of sugar. Brix is another measure of sugar.

Big: A wine full of flavour and high in alcohol, tannin, acidity and extract.

Bitter: A taste term; registers at the back of the mouth.

Body: Weight of wine in the mouth due to its alcoholic content, extract and other components.

Bodega: A wine cellar.

Bouquet: The part of the **nose** which comes from the fermentation and ageing processes.

Brix: (Bricks) or Balling. A hydrometer calibrated measure of sugar used mainly in the USA and NZ.

Brut: Drier type of sparkling wine.

Capsule: Covering for top of bottle - made from plastic, tin, foil or wax - to protect against leaking, borers and refilling. Improves appearance of bottle.

Caramel: A slightly burnt, toffee-like flavour.

Carbon dioxide: Responsible for the bubbles in sparkling wines and the tingle of spritzig or effervescent table wines.

Character: Smell and flavour term - referring to vinosity and style.

Clean: Wine free of off-flavours or tastes.

Clone: A sub-variety or strain that has developed within a particular grape variety.

Cloudy: Suspended matter in solution, turbid, obscuring clarity and color.

Cloying: A sweet or heavy wine lacking the acidity to make it crisp.

Coarse: Rough texture; lacking style and poor fruit or processing.

Corky: A distinct earthy smell of cork, arising from bacteria in the cork.

Crisp: Usually refers to white wines of good acidity that stimulate the taste sense. Normally a characteristic of grapes grown in cool climates.

Dessert wine: Taken at the end of a meal, e.g. port, liqueur muscat, sweeter sherry styles.

Developed: A maturity stage, balanced, rounded, at its best.

Dry: Opposite to sweet - not wet - without sugar.

Dull: 1. Appearance - not bright; 2. nose and in-mouth lacking interest.

Dumb: Undeveloped but with inherent promise of quality. Often the sign of an adolescent stage.

Earthy: Characteristic smell and flavour derived from certain soils containing the chemical geosmin.

Enology: U.S. spelling of oenology.

Elevage: Literally raising; describes the operations of maturing and blending young wines to attain better balance and quality.

Estate-bottled: Bottled at the winery adjoining the vineyards where the grapes were grown. Local interpretations have broadened this original meaning.

Ethyl alcohol: The purest alcohol - not poisonous to the human system; a product of fermented grape juice.

Fat: Full body, high in glycerol and extract.

Fermentation: The miracle of turning grape juice to wine. Yeast enzymes convert grape sugars to ethyl alcohol and carbon dioxide.

Fermentation, alcoholic: Transformation of the sugar contained in the must, into alcohol and carbon dioxide, in the presence of yeasts.

Fermentation, malolactic: Follows the alcoholic fermentation. Malic acid is affected by specific bacteria and changed into lactic acid and carbon dioxide. Because lactic acid is less harsh than malic acid, when young the wine becomes softer and more pleasant to drink.

Filtering: Process of separation of unwanted elements such as lees or dead yeast from the wine.

Fining: Way of clearing wines before they are bottled. With this method a colloid is added to the wine to absorb suspended particles and to fall with gravity to the bottom of the container. Products used are beaten egg white, fish glue, casein or bentonite, a type of clay. The wine is then drawn off and usually filtered before bottling.

Finish: Last impression left in the mouth by the wine - the "memory".

Firm: Positive in the mouth.

Flabby: Too much fruit, too little acid and usually coarse.

Flat: Sparkling wine that has lost its bubbles - or a dull and uninteresting still wine usually lacking acid.

Flowery: Pleasantly aromatic - in young white wines with freshness.

Fortified: Refers to wines with added grape spirit, e.g. port, sherry, marsala.

Fruity: Aroma and flavour of fresh grapes or other fruits.

Free run: Unpressed juice or wine drawn off before, during or after fermentation.

Generic: Wine names which refer to historic or geographic areas, e.g. burgundy, moselle, sherry

Green: Common to taste and smell - excessive grape acid - sharp flavour.

Grip: A firm combination of physical characteristics, mainly tannin.

Hard: Dry, almost bitter, unpleasant, too much acid and/or tannin.

Heady: Wines high in alcohol.

Hectare: One hundred square metres, the equivalent of 2.47 acres.

Hedonistic: A simple subjective, personal rating, eg pleasant to the individual.

Late picked: Wine made from grapes left longer on vines to reach high sugar levels - see Spatlese.

Lees: Made up of latent yeasts, tartars and residual matter from the fruit. The lees forms a deposit at the bottom of the cask. These are removed during racking.

Light: A confusing term that can apply to the alcoholic strength of a wine. A full-bodied wine can be light on flavour.

Limpid: Clear (appearance).

Long: Lingering flavour; a sign of quality.

Magnum: A large bottle with a capacity of 1.5 litres or the equivalent of two ordinary bottles. Fine wines are more slowly aged in magnums than in 750 ml bottles.

Malic Acid: An acid from grapes and green apples which leaves a puckering sensation in the mouth.

Marc: The residue of skins and seeds after juice is extracted by pressing.

Nose: Combines the aroma and bouquet.

Oenology: The science of wine production.

Palate: The hard roof of the mouth which has no taste receptors, a misnomer when used for wine evaluation.

Spicy: Wines of pronounced varietal character, muscat and traminer are good examples.

Sulphury: Generally refers to sulfur (sulphur) dioxide - the most common antiseptic in wine making.

Supple: Mouth-filling, easy to drink.

Tactile: The touch sense.

Tannin: A natural substance in grape skins, seeds and oak casks. Provides the "backbone" in red wine.

Tart: Possessing agreeable high acidity from the natural fruit acid.

Threshold: Level at which a given smell or taste can be perceived. Thresholds vary from person to person, from substance to substance.

Thin: Lack of body, watery.

Tinto: Red.

Ullage: The space between the wine and the cork, or wine and top of cask.

Varietal: Wine made from a single grape variety.

Veraison: The time when the fruit changes color during ripening.

Wood: Refers to oak casks of varying size.

BIBLIOGRAPHY

CATALONIA - Traditions, Places, Wine & Food
Jan Read & Maite Manjón - Herbert 1992

WINES & CAVES - Denominació d'Origen Penedès - undated

MIL AÑOS DE VITICULTURA EN CATALUÑYA
Edivisa 1990

A PRACTICAL AMPELOGRAPHY
Grapevine Identification - Cornell 1979

THE NEW WINES OF SPAIN - Tony Lord
Wine Appreciation Guild - 1988

GUIDE TO WINE GRAPES - Jancis Robinson
Oxford University Press - 1996

THE WINE ATLAS OF SPAIN - Hubrecht Duijker
Simon & Schuster - 1992

PENEDÈS, el Vi - 2nd Edition - Novaprint SA 1997

WINE IS FUN - Alan Young
International Wine Academy - 1996

THE NEW SPAIN - John Radford - Mitchell Beazley 1998

PHOTO CREDITS

Harold Heckle - end pages, page 64, 90, 140
Restaurant Ca la Katy - pages 160, 162, 164, 166, 168, 170.
Miguel Torres SA - page 108
Alan Young - pages 14, 16, 23, 32, 34-44, 48, 56, 58, 60, 62, 64, 69, 70, 72, 74, 76, 79, 80, 82, 84, 88, 90, 92, 94, 96, 98, 99, 102, 104, 106, 110, 112, 116, 120, 122, 126, 128, 130, 132, 135, 136, 140, 142, 144, 146.

INDEX